on track ...

Green Day

every album, every song

William E. Spevack

SONIC**BOND**

sonicbondpublishing.com

Sonicbond Publishing Limited
www.sonicbondpublishing.co.uk
Email: info@sonicbondpublishing.co.uk

First Published in the United Kingdom 2023
First Published in the United States 2023

British Library Cataloguing in Publication Data:
A Catalogue record for this book is available from the British Library

ISBN 978-1-78952-261-7

Typeset in ITC Garamond Std & ITC Avant Garde Gothic Pro
Printed and bound in England

Graphic design and typesetting: Full Moon Media

on track ...

Green Day

every album, every song

William E. Spevack

SONICBOND

sonicbondpublishing.com

This book is dedicated to my mom, who passed away weeks after I began writing it. She was excited to know it was for a band she enjoyed. Despite her older age, she didn't mind rocking out to Green Day and was very supportive. She served as a big inspiration for me to continue and complete this enjoyable endeavor. Mom, I love you and miss you, and this book is for you. Rest in peace Dianne Spevack.

Acknowlegements

Thanks to Stephen Lambe for giving me this opportunity. This has been a fantastic journey and your feedback has been a huge help throughout the process. Thanks also to Peter Kearns, the editor who greatly improved this book. Both of you have been invaluable to me in this unforgettable experience.

And thanks to Helga Spevack, Keith Koncurat, Dareth McKenna, Monte Large, Frantz Andersen, Holly Lown, Yuliya Alterman, and my Bard professors, particularly Donna Ford Grover.

Foreword: Green Day, The Radio Revolutionaries

Green Day is an incredibly successful band, critically and commercially. Singer/guitarist Billie Joe Armstrong, bassist Mike Dirnt and drummer Tré Cool have been together creating rock music with a punk heart for over three decades. The trio has reigned supreme, shattering previously-conceived notions about how commercially successful a punk-rock band can be, and helping extend the boundaries of the genre. For three decades, Green Day bounced off the wide walls of alternative rock's creativity with a passion and fire that ignited some of rock's greatest albums. According to Joel Whitburn's Rock Tracks 1981-2008, Green Day, at that point, was ranked as the third overall most successful rock band on the Billboard Modern Rock charts, behind only the Red Hot Chili Peppers and U2. They also ranked third all-time on that chart for most top tens and most number one's. They revolutionized 1990s punk by installing brilliant melodic pop songwriting infused with their sneering and snotty youthful. The following decade, they expanded their alternative rock sound so widely that they became one of the few bands in history to inspire a second generation of youthful fans through a different style of rock music.

In Rodeo, California, in the 1980s, singer/guitarist Billie Joe Armstrong and bassist Mike Dirnt were just kids out to have some fun. By the 1990s, through massive sales and commercial appeal, the group – who'd drummer Tré Cool at the start of the decade – fueled a firestorm of new pop-punk bands that crashed into the mainstream. The biggest-selling punk album of all-time – 1994's *Dookie* – was the centerpiece of the new punk revolution. Despite backlash from the indie punk community, who thought Green Day was selling out, the band continued to successfully blast through more of their influential pop-punk sound, inspiring hundreds of bands around the world.

After perfecting their formula, by the turn of the century, Green Day challenged themselves to push past punk's aural barriers and embrace their love for classic rock, folk rock, power pop and straight pop, opening their musical and lyrical minds, to create more ambitious works. After they cleared the slate of their older works by releasing a greatest hits album and a B-sides compilation in the early-2000s, the band set themselves up for maximum stardom.

With tremendous ambition, they took on the category of the rock opera. 2004's *American Idiot* was the result of Armstrong's idea of how it felt to live as a youth in America in the 2000s. Heavily politicized and socially aware, the concept album's alternative-rock style struck a chord with a new set of fans growing up with teenage angst and a distrust for politicians. The record became successful and critically acclaimed. The massive thematic scope continued with a second concept album – 2009's *21st Century Breakdown* – which successfully navigated similarly troubled waters on social, political and personal levels.

By the 2010s, Green Day had reset their strategy. Feeling nostalgic, the trio looked to rekindle their early, non-thematic pop-punk songwriting, feeding it with garage rock, through their brief side project band Foxboro Hot Tubs. Green Day issued the trio of records *¡Uno!*, *¡Dos!* and *¡Tré!*. The new albums stalled their momentum some, but by then, their legacy was set. In 2015, Green Day was inducted into The Rock N' Roll Hall Of Fame, and re-established their credibility as one of the world's best rock bands by unleashing some of their greatest songs and performances to create the stimulating *Revolution Radio*.

In the 2020s, Green Day is still a band in high demand for tens of millions of fans. This book tracks how their music progressed from their indie days, through their rock operas, to their most recent material. It dissects every song from every album.

on track ...
Green Day

Contents

Introduction

In 1977, punk was on the minds of many. But there was a five-year-old who was not in tune with the punk rock world. Billie Joe Armstrong had talent and was ready to let loose when his mother, Ollie, loaded him into the car to take him to a recording studio. When they were at parties, she'd recognized that little Billie Joe could sing well.

He was born the youngest of six children on 17 February 1972 in Oakland, California. By 1977, he recorded a song called 'Look For Love,' written by James J. and Marie Louise Fiatarone. It was pressed for Fiat Records with James producing. Billie Joe's recording was soft rock with a tint of light jazz. But in the year that punk popped, the Sex Pistols were singing 'Anarchy In The U.K.,' and The Clash were singing 'Hate And War.' Tiny Billie Joe and his little female backing group predicted Green Day's early path of marrying love with punk. The B-side was a short interview with Billie Joe that had him dreaming of being in a rock band and making people happy with his music. A snippet of the interview was added to the intro of the Green Day song 'Maria' found on *International Superhits*. Not too surprisingly, Billie Joe loved rock 'n' roll much more than the light-jazz ballad he sang in 1972, and he particularly loved punk. In 1982, Armstrong's father, Andy, died from cancer. Ollie remarried later, but Billie Joe didn't like his stepfather.

Advancing time another five years, the 15-year-old Billie Joe was playing music with his 15-year-old friend Mike Pritchard. Michael Ryan Pritchard's rough childhood was enough to drive him into his own teen angst since his parents were divorced and his mother had drug addiction issues. Michael was an only child, born on 4 May 1972 in Oakland, California. His tough situation inspired him to pick up his guitar and rock out the pain, when he wasn't working to help the family make ends meet. By befriending his fellow Pinole Valley schoolmate Billie Joe, Mike had both a place to live and a place in a band. Despite both guitarists dealing with life as youths from a broken home, Billie Joe and Mike were on the right path, and while heading towards their future musical careers, their pals – bassist Sean Hughes and drummer Raj Punjabi – helped them out. They would write music together, where Billie Joe would be forthright with his opinions on relationships and sing about how he pined for girls that were just out of his reach. Relative to the East Bay punk scene, Green Day were *sweet children* singing about innocence, growing up and waiting for first kisses.

Naming themselves Sweet Children and beginning to play live shows in late 1987, Sean Hughes and Raj Punjabi eventually faded off back into their own lives, and older teen drummer John Kiffmeyer entered the fray. He was born on 11 May 1969 in El Sobrante, California. He adopted the nickname Al Sobrante, and would eventually be credited that way on some Green Day releases. John had played in a band before – Isocracy – and had more experience in the local music scene than Armstrong or Dirnt. Once he joined

Sweet Children, John was able to help them make more social connections, and the band grew prominently in the East Bay. Without a bassist, Mike had to switch from guitar to bass. Anytime he was pretending to play bass, he made a *dirnt dirnt* sound, which is how he acquired his stage name, Mike Dirnt. The band's lineup and sound were set.

The majority of their 1990s work was to come in bite-size, three-minute nuggets that were easily digested and highly addictive. Many songs would speed like a motorcycle towards the three-minute mark, fast enough to toss listeners into the road. Though the listeners may have been bruised from the speed and aggression, the band's music, fortified – the almost-roadkill audience were satisfied, excited, and motivated enough to get up, dust themselves off and jump onto the next speeding motorcycle-like song shooting towards them. Billie Joe grew more comfortable writing lyrics, improving on every new platter Green Day released from 1989 through to 2004.

The band's live shows were fresh and lively enough to gain the attention of small-time local music executive Larry Livermore, who'd co-founded Lookout Records with his friend David Hayes. Livermore – a musician himself in the band The Lookouts (featuring future-Green Day drummer Tré Cool) – signed Sweet Children to a recording contract. In Green Day's 1994 interview with MTV's *120 Minutes*, Tré Cool spoke of the band's 1988 signing: 'I lived in the middle of nowhere, and I called their old drummer (Al Sobrante) and asked them to come play this party. I told him, 'Look, there's gonna be no one there except this guy Larry, which is the guy that does Lookout. There's gonna be a few kids.' Mike continued the tale: 'It was the deciding factor, and how we based our friendship too, and how we really got to know each other. We smoked a lot of pot up there, and just played in a freezing cold place with no roof and a generator. After three songs, all these guys wanted to leave. They were like, 'Can you move your van?' and we're like, 'No, you're staying for the show. There's 11 of you here and we drove 20,000 hours to get here'.' Billie Joe added: 'The woman running the show wasn't there, so we broke into the house. It wasn't even a signing thing. It was just like, 'Well, you want to do a 7-inch?'

Sweet Children entered a recording studio for the first time to record their first EP. The band decided that a name change was needed to avoid possible mix-ups with local band Sweet Baby. As many fans know, Sweet Children changed their name to Green Day simply based on their love of marijuana. But there were still no psychedelic, druggy vibes, as the band were known to enjoy harder music like AC/DC, Van Halen, Black Sabbath, Husker Dü, The Replacements, and fellow labelmates – and one of their biggest influences – Operation Ivy. Still, unlike other punk rockers of the day, Green Day enjoyed other rock acts that weren't always hard-edged, like The Beatles, Elvis Presley, The Who, Queen, Bruce Springsteen and R.E.M. Billie Joe's influences were rooted in what came from his parents and his five siblings.

In a 1990 interview with *Flipside,* the band explained how they figured out what music they wanted to play, by elimination. Billie Joe stated:

> Well yeah, it just evolved. We tried a few different things, and we got sick of the whole heavy metal thing, because it wasn't that interesting. We didn't really have the taste to be a hardcore band, so we started doing this. Yeah, I couldn't really sing about destroying the government or anything like that, because I don't know much about it. It's not our style, so we don't write them. There're girls out there.

Billie Joe reflected on old times with Larry Livermore in a 2009 interview reuniting the two: 'The funny thing was, everything we were doing, we were being heartfelt about. We were singing love songs because that's what we felt like. That's what was in my heart. And I think that creeps people out a little bit. Vulnerability really creeps people out.'

For their two indie albums and three indie EPs, Green Day wrote and sung about love with a reflective, vulnerable attitude typically found in softer music. When tying-in their distorted guitar tones, tough rhythms and brash musical attitude, they created a workable dichotomy. Their hooky, singable vocal melodies ramped up the resonance of their songs' intentions. The songs consisted of a hit-'n'-run of just two verses, a chorus, a brief intro and coda. Musically, the focus was strictly propulsive punk with only a guitar, bass, drums and Billie Joe's vocal, set in a thin indie-rock production.

Green Day performed mostly pop-punk for the 1990s, sometimes leaning towards metal riffs, sometimes straight punk. Bassist Mike Dirnt was playing simpler than he would later, and drummer John Kiffmeyer was creative enough to keep the songs stimulating. But the overall band performance was stifled by the poor studio recording. Decades later, new generations of teen fans go on YouTube and express how Billie Joe knows them and their lives. The lyrics aren't challenging but resonate richly across age groups and generations. Fans can feel like they're Green Day's buddy or group therapist.

Rocking venues in East Bay, with some of their time spent at Tim Yohannan's club at 924 Gilman in Berkeley, California, Green Day continued to write songs and gain a consistent audience. Livermore felt it was time to gather the group together for the recording session, directing them to producer/engineer Andy Ernst at Art-Of-Ears studio in San Francisco.

1000 Hours (EP) (1989)

Personnel:
Billie Joe Armstrong: lead vocals, guitar
Mike Dirnt: bass, backing vocals
John Kiffmeyer: drums
Producer: Andy Ernst
Recorded at Art-Of-Ears studio, San Francisco, California
Label: Lookout
Release date: May 26, 1989
Chart: US: –

Recorded in just seven hours, Green Day's *1000 Hours* EP was direct, simple, and a fine outing for these 16-year-olds. It acts like a short play about a teen boy in his bedroom dreaming about a girl. The protagonist assumes she doesn't have a crush on him, let alone any feelings of love, and once the EP is flipped to the B-side, we find out his theory was correct. Side B keeps the listener in the bedroom as the teen boy tries unsuccessfully to suppress his unrequited desire. Several Green Day biographies point to a friend of Billie Joe's sister named Jennifer as being the target of Billie Joe's infatuation. She was older than him, and unwilling to date the young, somewhat-naïve schoolkid. Billie Joe finally confirmed it in 2014 when he tweeted, 'All the songs from the *1000 Hours* 7" are about the same girl.'

Dreaming and daydreaming are the themes. 'The one I love that I've been dreaming of' is a line in '1000 Hours.' 'Late last night I had a dream and she was in it again' and 'Oh I love her, keep dreaming of her' are lines in 'Dry Ice.' 'Many nights awake I lie' displays the restlessness of 'Only Of You.' Many more nights of worry, carpet-bomb Billie Joe's thoughts with insomnia in 'The One I Want' with another three mentions – 'Sitting in my room late last night,' 'All these long and sleepless nights' and 'Every night, I'm thinking about the words you say' exhibit Billie Joe's thoughts of love changing him into a sleep-deprived, nocturnal being that pines for Jennifer.

Side A

'1000 Hours' (Lyric: Armstrong; Music: Green Day)

The romantic '1000 Hours' starts with a sweet (as children) melody. The guitar buzzes reliably, with the bass and drums along for the ride. Many of Green Day's earliest sonic adventures were recorded at Art-of-Ears studio, and Armstrong's guitar sounds like a thin, sustained line of distortion, with strums and individual notes swallowed. It completes with cascading guitar smashed up by Al Sobrante's final crashing drum fills.

This might as well be the sweet anthem of the ex-Sweet Children, as it's the only openly-optimistic song here – revealing innocence and naivete; free from the burdens of life and love. Armstrong yearns with a youthful enthusiasm, and by the end of 1000 hours – or a little over 41 days – he knows that their love trance will happily bind them forever in this 'love shower.'

'Dry Ice' (Lyric: Armstrong; Music: Green Day)
This metallic pop/rock tune has the type of brisk and bright mid-tempo pace that doesn't quite match hardcore punk's speed but presents its power. Billie Joe pulls off an effective guitar part, and the band's first vocal harmonies (Armstrong and Dirnt) are evident on the melodically worthwhile chorus.

'Dry Ice' might as well have frozen Green Day's pessimistic mindset for the next decade, as they forego the sweet possibilities found in '1000 Hours' for a sour reflection on love. The narrator is in his bedroom, awoken by a cold sweat, as he realizes his dream is over – and with it, his imaginary romance.

Side B
'Only Of You' (Lyric: Armstrong; Music: Green Day)
The metallic sneer of 'Only Of You' employs Mike's natural bass-playing gift for its sunny melody, set under Billie Joe's jet stream of guitar distortion. After a brief vocal-harmony section, our guitarist whips up another fine guitar solo. The sunny melody and joyous singing, match his appreciation for Jennifer.

Back in his bedroom reality, Billie Joe pictures himself conveying to Jennifer that he doesn't know how to properly communicate his attraction. He feels it's love at first sight but then must wrestle with himself, knowing that the feelings are not mutual.

'The One I Want' (Lyric: Armstrong, Dirnt; Music: Green Day)
The *metalheads* here continue favoring metal tones with punk speed. It's a loud and meaty up-tempo pop-punk sound with grunge-level guitar distortion. The chorus and verse contain major-league hooks – something that would later set Green Day apart from just about every punk band and most alternative rock bands. They were ranked sixth on *Billboard*'s list of most successful Modern Rock bands of the 1990s according to *Rock Tracks 1981-2008*. Billie Joe and Mike join to cement the chorus hooks vocally. An extended jangly guitar solo lifts the mood considerably and feeds the piece's romantic root.

For this final tune, we find our fallen narrator grieving in his bedroom as he examines his reflection in the mirror, trying to wrap his head around her let's-be-friends rejection. In this anti-climactic final act of the *1000 Hours* love saga, Billie Joe's craving never says die as he repeats the song title several times, judging that if he can stay persistent with the thought, someday it might come true.

39/Smooth (1990)

Personnel:
Billie Joe Armstrong: lead vocals, guitar
Mike Dirnt: bass, backing vocals
John Kiffmeyer: drums, percussion, backing vocals
Producer: Andy Ernst, Green Day
Recorded at Art Of Ears studio, San Francisco, California
Label: Lookout
Release date: 13 April 1990
Chart: US: –

'Here we go again/Infatuation touches me/Just when I thought that it was ending,' Billie Joe busts out vocally on 'Going To Pasalacqua,' wearing his heart on his sleeve for a second record. Green Day's debut album is like the *1000 Hours* EP musically and lyrically, yet the odd title was too obscure a reference for a fan to guess at. Mike Dirnt explained to *Flipside* in 1990: 'It's named after Billie's brother because we recorded it on the day he turned 39, but he's a smooth character.'

The brevity of the recording sessions indicated how the band knew the songs completely, taking them from the stage to the studio. They needed just 22 hours to finish the album over the last days of 1989 and opening days of 1990. They were now familiar with the recording studio, and knew producer/engineer Andy Ernst, who'd already recorded their debut EP, which only cost $675 to record.

Musically they continued down the exact path started on *1,000 Hours*, performing concise lo-fi pop-punk songs fast and loud with plenty of guitar distortion. Generally, the vocal melodies are the strongest feature since the arrangements are simple. The lyrics are elementary though resonant, and the band is not ambitious in any way – lacking flair and dynamics. They get into the song, stick to the song, and get out. Lyrically, Billie Joe is pining for a girl – playing his role as the teen lovebird protagonist.

39/Smooth was issued on vinyl in 1990 and reissued on CD in 1991 with their first two EPs *1000 Hours* and *Slappy* – the latter recorded a week after the album was released. The 1991 compilation *1039 Smoothed Out Slappy Hours* has sold 2,000,000 copies worldwide and was certified gold in the US and UK.

Side A

'At The Library' (Armstrong, Dirnt, Kiffmeyer)

Billie Joe Armstrong would rather read women's looks than books. Going to the library and then singing about it with your punk-rock fans listening is a common tradition – but only in an alternate universe! 'At The Library' is like a book you can't put down. The verses and choruses are so catchy, and the

15

nerdy bookworm lyrics bleed indie emo. It's an irresistible slice of punky pop/rock. Dirnt's bass, flirts with the vocal melody, and Kiffmeyer holds steady, only slowing down for the brief bridge.

The track represents Green Day's younger days well. Usually, punk-music teen tales are pimply, puss-filled pissing matches attempting to see which ear of a listener they can deafen first. But 'At The Library' has none of the vocal aggression – just a 17-year-old kid singing about hanging out in the library to get his school work done, instead peering over his textbook to eye that special someone he's targeting for romance. Our protagonist is out of luck as her boyfriend arrives to pick her up, and they leave the library together. 'What makes me feel so much pain that makes me go insane?,' Billie Joe sings even before his library love leaves with her beau. If we were to use the library's system, it's as if the singer can borrow a book like he borrowed eye contact, but can never keep the book or the girl. Oddly, the song is listed with the subtitle 'With Waba Sé Wasca.' The subtitle was dropped when 'At the Library' was listed for the compilation. Though Billie Joe wrote the lyric, John Kiffmeyer lived the tale, as he told *Flipside* in 1990: 'Yo, I went through literally the exact thing that happened in the song. There's this girl a grade above me. She's really pretty, I wanted to go up to her and start talking to her, but I could never figure out what to say or the right time to say anything. Just recently, I found out she's dating my friend's friend.'

'Don't Leave Me' (Armstrong, Dirnt, Kiffmeyer)

More metallic shards fly out at the listeners when they hear the speedy 'Don't Leave Me,' but they can dodge the pieces as they headbang to another resonant rhythm. Kiffmeyer drills in the beat like a construction worker, Dirnt goes the forceful punk bass route, and Armstrong sends out long streams of aggressive guitar. Unfortunately, the verse melody isn't strong, and there's no hook on the refrain – Billie Joe spitting out words without shaping the words to the music. The stop/start dynamics here would remain a crucial element in the band's sound, but double-tracked vocals would be replaced by Mike Dirnt's harmonies.

The narrator finds himself in a troubled relationship, like when two love birds are no longer singing but chirping about misery. 'I feel my mind is going insane' continues the active sanity gauge.

'I Was There' (Lyrics: Kiffmeyer; Music: Armstrong, Dirnt, Kiffmeyer)

This choice is a bright, optimistic number holding one of the album's best melodies. The quirky guitar solo leaps from 1960s rock to metal, Mike joins in vocally, and Al Sobrante is voraciously hungry on drums, adding dramatic cymbal crashes on the choruses. The tempo change into the bridge and Dirnt's praiseworthy bass effort on the coda, are highlights.

The band works up the tune, and Kiffmeyer writes a poignant reflection on his youth. Many fans picked up on the irony of early nostalgic feelings from such a young band. Kiffmeyer told *Flipside* in 1990: 'It's about being sad about the past. It's not saying it was better back then, it's just your frame of reference.'

Unlike so many that remember their youth through rose-colored glasses, Kiffmeyer understood the balance of the past, present and future, and his confidence shone through on lyrics like, 'There's no doubt about who I am, I always have tomorrow.' Al Sobranté – as John was nicknamed – is sure his future will provide many more memorable moments and people. The faith in the future and the platter of experience, is a major contrast to Billie Joe's innocent songs of pessimism. Sobranté wrote a song of experience, while Armstrong wrote songs of inexperience.

'Disappearing Boy' (Armstrong, Dirnt, Kiffmeyer)
The melodic 'Disappearing Boy' has a chorus hook that slowly pierces our skin before digging into the flesh as it heads to the bone. In other words, it's one of their first massively-irresistible hooks. They smartly slow down for the bridge, so Armstrong can get reflective before going quiet like his guitar. The song kicks back into gear with a solo-less guitar break, before double-timing back towards one final fantastic chorus go-around. Dirnt is somewhat quiet, allowing space for Kiffmeyer's busy playing.

Though the song could be about that library girl from 'At The Library,' with lines like 'I see her and she's with him/I turn around and then I'm gone,' the protagonist is opening his world further for listeners to visit. He feels like that ignored womanless wallflower at parties, and begins to wonder where he belongs in life. 'I vanished from all your joy/When I walk in crowded rooms/I feel as if it's my doom/I know I don't belong,' implies he's more comfortable in the library.

'Green Day' (Armstrong, Dirnt, Kiffmeyer)
Yes, it's Green Day's officially-sanctioned anthem, with an intro swimming in bubbling-bong sound effects. But there's a reason why it's not one of their most well-known or acclaimed tracks – it's lacking lyrically and melodically, hanging its hat on a serviceable verse hook. After a mediocre breakdown and guitar noodle, it's back with force into the punkish heart of this ode to pot. There's no psychedelia within its walls.

Kiffmeyer may be the star of the song, relying on lots of drum rolls for a mighty effort. Still very new to lyric writing, Billie Joe doesn't provoke much visually with his 'White mist hits the ground' and 'Sounds of moving insects' lines, eventually tying them to a woman he's attracted to. Billie Joe told *Time*:

I wrote a song called 'Green Day' because I was smoking a lot of dope. It's basically a song about staring up at the ceiling, thinking about a girl and being stoned. Our drummer put 'Green Day' on his jacket and said, 'Maybe we should call the band that', and I said, 'That's a good idea.'

Side B
'Going To Pasalacqua' (Armstrong, Dirnt, Kiffmeyer)

This propulsive and exhilarating song has one of Green Day's greatest intros. Billie Joe sings, 'Here we go again,' unable to hold his emotion before the band smashes us in the face with their most confident, aggressive playing; a thunderous, rousing performance, surfing on fantastic hooks. The awe-inspiring combination of melody and power, shows their talent and potential. A fun, uptempo, pop-punk track with metallic flourishes that hit all the right spots, it's another album highlight. The band continually double-down after a one-second-long pause on the phrase 'Far away,' separating it from the rest of the chorus like it's far away from the rest of the refrain.

'Going to Pasalacqua' is a live favorite, a fan favorite, and one of the most significant summaries of the various blood vessels that run through the Green Day body. Billie Joe is realizing the lovelorn pattern when he charges out of the gate like a Kentucky Derby horse, with the signature line of the band's indie-rock career: 'Here we go again/Infatuation touches me just when I thought that it would end.' The repetition of heart struck then heart broken dominates Green Day's indie music.

'Well, I toss and turn all night thinking of your ways of affection,' Armstrong complains, like he's done before, describing more lonely bedroom scenes, more insomnia, more attempts to perfect his pitch of romance. He was always more aware of his timeline than the typical teen. In the pre-chorus, he sings about leaving the errors of his old ways behind, and decides, 'What the hey?' Why not try again? The heart rehabilitation has fully completed from his last stress, in the most exciting performance on *39/Smooth*.

'16' (Armstrong, Dirnt, Kiffmeyer)

The quality comedown to '16' isn't so agonizing, but it's a comedown from 'Going To Pasalacqua'. Some of the youth and amateur feelings they talk of during '16' are evident in the performance. The rhythm is a bit off, the guitar isn't particularly creative, and Armstrong's vocal is loose but still carries emotion. The band's strongest value – their vocal melody and hooks – are mostly in hiding during '16,' though Dirnt provides exemplary bass creativity.

The old expression goes, 'Youth is wasted on the young', but life for a teen can be tough, and it was an era in which teenage angst stormed the airwaves. The following year, Nirvana's *Nevermind*, Pearl Jam's *Ten*, and Soundgarden's *Badmotorfinger* were vital grunge albums that felt relatable to teens. Green Day's lyrics would lose some of their innocence as the decade wore on and sometimes paralleled the grunge movement. Here Green Day serves up a new dish to deal with for the next few years – the thoughts of growing up and wondering about an adult future. 'Every night I dream the same dream of getting older and older every time,' Billie Joe sings, as we find ourselves sitting in a chair next to his bed, playing therapist.

'Road To Acceptance' (Armstrong, Dirnt, Kiffmeyer)

This thoughtful song is the first of many times that Green Day share societal insight. The singsong pre-chorus is alright, but the main refrain is admirable. Dirnt stays mellow, so Kiffmeyer goes loud with lots of bass drum and cymbal hits on the verses, until he slides over for Dirnt to raise his profile for the chorus, instrumental break and bridge.

After a brief intimate Billie Joe moment, the band's familiar uptempo, bright and confident rhythm prevails, though they can't quite nail the melody. *39/Smooth* could use *more* exciting dynamics like the bass-and-drum breakdown that provides a midsection spark.

The band's early material was soaked in the need to be accepted by women. But 'Road To Acceptance' is about those who aren't accepted because of prejudice. In a 1990 concert currently available on YouTube, Billie Joe introduces the song with this line: 'This song's about racist pigs, and I think that anyone who wants to fuck with someone cause of the color of their skin is....' He then contorts his face into an ugly, angry and disgusted look. Though he sings about himself in verse one – 'I'll sculpt my life for your acceptance' – he's only using himself as one example of the millions of lives sculpted and tailored for others' acceptance. (The individualist theme will come back in force for *Warning*, *American Idiot*, and *21st Century Breakdown*.) By verse two, he branches out, citing the pain felt by so many who are ostracized.

'Rest' (Armstrong, Dirnt, Kiffmeyer)

Neither punk nor metal, the grunge of 'Rest' fits right into the scene above California in the Northwest more than the rest of Green Day's catalog. It has a lazy sound, especially considering it's the only slow song from the band's Lookout Records era. But with the massive tempo change comes a massive hole in quality. Armstrong had his purposely-tired vocals multitracked, and the sluggish feel is suitable but provides little entertainment. They'd do *slow* songs a lot better years later.

Billie Joe, the insomniac, weighs his chances with a woman he desires. The 'angel' living in verse two 'dances away,' getting him excited. But then she 'turns away,' leaving him unsure whether she likes him or not. It results in another bedroom scene, with our protagonist lying in bed, working involuntarily on the dilemma, with an unsettled mind. 'Rest' is usually considered to be the album's low moment.

'The Judge's Daughter' (Armstrong, Dirnt, Kiffmeyer)

Here the band go back to uptempo pop-punk, highlighted by the suspenseful bridge that leads into one of Billie Joe's best guitar solos. In places, he adds a vocal harmony.

The song is about another Billie Joe crush on a girl who figuratively crushes him. Yet this time, he puts the blame on her instead of considering himself crazy. It's a rare early lyric that finds our lovebird in a relationship already, but his eyes are wandering towards the girl he really wants. Usually, Armstrong's present-tense notions are in a second-person voice. But here, he changes the second chorus to progress the story: 'My girlfriend left me on the phone/I'm pathetically left here alone/I cannot call this sane,' he declares once more from his bedroom in heartache land.

Slappy (EP) (1990)

Personnel:
Billie Joe Armstrong: lead vocals, guitar
Mike Dirnt: bass, backing vocals
John Kiffmeyer: drums
Additional personnel:
Aaron Cometbus: backing vocals; teeth ('Knowledge')
Producers: Andy Ernst, Green Day
Recorded at Art Of Ears studio, San Francisco, California
Label: Lookout
Release date: 1990
Chart: US: –

Just days after *39/Smooth* was issued, Green Day were back in Art Of Ears studio in San Francisco with Andy Ernst (listed as 'Andro') to quickly record their second EP *Slappy*, completing it in a single day. Their friend Jason Relva named his dog Slappy. Relva would be the subject of Green Day's 1995 song 'J.A.R.'

Billie Joe tweeted, 'The songs that were on the *Slappy* EP – songs like '409' and 'Paper Lanterns,' 'Why Do You Want Him?' – We felt like we were moving, like we were coming into our own.' Musically, the band are in typical pop-punk mode. Their signature sound had already been set on their first EP, and it continued in that vein throughout most of the 1990s, with some notable exceptions. One exception on *Slappy* is 'Knowledge,' which removes the constant guitar distortion living in their other tracks, adding harmonica, silly vocals and some much-needed sonic space. Lyrically, the first half of the EP is like a photocopy of their previous love songs. Billie Joe craves romance.

Side A

'Paper Lanterns' (Lyrics: Armstrong; Music: Green Day)

The crunchy 'Paper Lanterns' continues their pop-punk stance. They blend the verse into the chorus with a singular melody. Luckily, they come through with potent musicality, but the metallic guitar solo isn't Armstrong's best. Dirnt continues his melodic bass approach, lingering around the vocal melody, and John keeps it simple, landing on a lot of hi-hats and snare drums. It's one of the first times they play with their most popular toy: the stop/start dynamic.

'Paper Lanterns' continues the heartache of their early times – Billie Joe becoming obsessed with the theme, perhaps to heal his heart and relieve the pressure he put on himself to find the right relationship. Singing directly to the listener as his *friend* girl in the second-person, he sounds desperate as usual, asking, 'So when are all my troubles going to end?,' trying to accept that they're only friends. But he has no qualms about confessing, 'To this day, I'm asking why I still think about you.' Like his heart was a

21

paper lantern, it's fragile and burns with desire for a partner, becoming too hot to handle before it finally disappears in ash and smoke. While it's an analogy Armstrong is reaching for, on later songs, he was to gradually find better ways to represent his passions. The opening line about resting his head goes right back to the debut album's 'Rest,' but this time, he's accepted defeat.

'Why Do You Want Him?' (Lyrics: Armstrong; Music: Green Day)
The band continue to provide solid power-trio work on their speedy songs. The giddy-sounding rhythm is a mismatch with Billie Joe's whiny vocal. There's almost none of the aggression evident in most punk, and their singsong chorus sounds uniquely innocent. Armstrong surprises us with one of his best guitar solos, ripping up the rhythm but keeping things entertaining without straying away from the song. Kiffmeyer goes with toms, and Dirnt cooks up a glorious bass countermelody, topping Armstrong's bland vocal melody.

The first song Billie Joe ever wrote, 'Why Do You Want Him?' is rumored to be about his mother's then-new boyfriend that Billie Joe he didn't care for, but it's unclear. While it can be interpreted that way, what might fit best is the typical scenario of Billie Joe liking a girl who's in a relationship with someone else.

Side B
'409 In Your Coffeemaker' (Lyrics: Armstrong; Music: Green Day)
The band's playing is getting tighter, but there haven't been too many outstanding performances instrumentally. That's partially because Billie Joe's hooks are taking the attention. It's so easy to sing along to Armstrong's foggy-headed self-conscious lyrics. His great hook is accentuated by Mike's harmony on the refrain. They stop the rhythm completely, come back in sync with two notes, followed by silence each time, then continue again. Billie Joe re-enters to sing the bridge, finding spaces between the powerful guillotine slices of guitar, bass and drums. It's one of the band's few Lookout songs with three verses.

Flipping over the record finds Billie Joe in a classroom for Show-and-Tell day. But Billie's is reversed as he brings his listeners into class to reveal how boring school can be. His skeptical thoughts about his future – 'Maybe I'm just too damn lazy/Or maybe I was brainwashed to think that way' – reveal why he really dropped out of high school. The title stems from the nasty prank of pouring the liquid cleaning product Formula 409 into a school's coffee maker, probably located in the teacher's lounge. As a band favorite, the track saw a second release in 'unmixed' form for the B-side to their future 1994 single 'Basket Case.' It wasn't too different, but Billie Joe's vocals stand out more. Years later, he chose '409 In Your Coffeemaker' as a song that defined his life, as he told *Rolling Stone*:

I'd just dropped out of high school, and I was feeling really lost, like a daydreamer who was being left behind. I didn't know what life was going to be. I think that's when I'm at my most honest as a songwriter, when I'm feeling lost. So, I took this sad feeling and turned it into something that felt more empowering: 'My interests are longing to break through these chains/ These chains that control my future's aims.' My songs were about infatuation up until that point. This one felt like a different version of who I am. I remember when we first started playing it, people were really receptive to it, especially the punks that were on the scene at the time. We had put out our first album and an EP, but this is where I felt like I had really found my rhythm as a songwriter. I was 18 years old.

'Knowledge' (Lyrics: Jesse Michaels; Music: Operation Ivy)
For the first time, Green Day doesn't try to arrange a marriage between power and melody, just letting Operation Ivy's hooks and lighthearted fun side shine through for the entertainment. The rarest of moments happens when Armstrong whips out the harmonica, and a rock-'n' roll guitar solo further alleviates any anguish left from the depressing first-three songs.

Local contemporaries, punk band Operation Ivy had broken up in 1989, so their send-off was a Green Day cover of 'Knowledge' from their 1989 *Energy* album. 'Knowledge' was well-sequenced, considering it sits next to its future-thinking partner song '409 In Your Coffeemaker.' Both songs deal with the notion that schools molding minds is really just the oldie-moldy philosophy that a student has to choose the direction and subject they'll endeavor to thrive in for the rest of their life.

The fun 'All I know is that I don't know nothing!' sing-along chorus that transgresses the title, helped make the track a fan favorite. As a concert highlight in 1995, Green Day followed Operation Ivy's winning crowd-engagement idea where fans get up on stage, are given an instrument and rock out with the band. It breaks down the wall between performers and audience, and the band still use it at shows with various songs over 25 years later. Billie Joe told *Spin* magazine in 2005: 'Everyone's got their band, and I've got to say Operation Ivy was definitely one that changed me.'

Sweet Children (EP) (1990)

Personnel:
Billie Joe Armstrong: lead vocals, guitar
Mike Dirnt: bass, backing vocals
John Kiffmeyer (listed as Al Sobrante): drums, backing vocals
Producer: Green Day
Recorded at Mac's Hole in the Ground (Six Feet Under), St. Paul, Minnesota
Label: Skene!
Release date: August 1990
Chart: US: -

Quickly recorded like all of the band's early material, their third EP *Sweet Children* was recorded on 5 July 1990 and issued a few months after *Slappy*. While it's unclear when the songs were written, they're painted with optimistic strokes. Life was getting better for Billie Joe in particular. He met his future – and still current – wife, Adrienne Nesser while in Minnesota. Obviously, she became a big inspiration for his writing in the future, but they wouldn't date just yet.

Armstrong pokes at his old love scars while continuing to wonder about what's ahead. The music is in the punk realm, so their aggressive guitar distortion, pumped-up drums and melodically-solid bass are a lot harder than their lyrics and personality. The contrast might be what made so many fans realize this was not your typical punk band – nor were they typical pop/rock or alternative rock.

Drummer John Kiffmeyer aka Al Sobrante, made his final recording with Green Day on *Sweet Children*. By 1991, he was gone, and soon after, Tré Cool from The Lookouts became the new drummer. He switched from Contra Costa College to Humboldt State University.

Side A (Listed as 'Side 1 Cup-o-mud')

'Sweet Children' (Lyrics: Armstrong; Music: Green Day)
This is another song that might've sounded better if they'd recorded it after jumping to a major label. The track shows the band's metallic side once again, but it stays firmly in the punk world. Billie Joe sounds like he's got a time bomb ticking next to him and has to rush out all the words before the instruments explode. At just 1:41 in length, it's one of Green Day's shortest songs, and we can barely comprehend the verse lyrics flying by. It's a shoddy number weakened by the lo-fi sound.

Playing the storyteller for the first time, Billie Joe weaves a tale about a blond virgin who is coaxed into having sex with a boy named Johnny Ray, who pressures her. After he takes advantage of her innocent sweetness, he's off wreaking havoc with a gun, committing the 'final sin.' The chorus just repeats the title, adding 'Remember when?,' referencing innocence lost.

It links back to '16,' where Armstrong wishes to be back in his innocent childhood days before dating.

'Best Thing In Town' (Lyrics: Armstrong, Dirnt; Music: Green Day)

The fun pop-punk 'Best Thing In Town' has turbo engines, and bursts out of the gate so fast that it's almost as if the band were already playing when Andy Ernst hit the record button. The coda guitar solo is strangled by its lack of room on the melodic scale but does the trick. The melody is suitably standard, but the chorus has a wonder of a motif. Dirnt and Kiffmeyer take a hit from the poor sound.

By summer 1990, Green Day were deciphering weed quality as marijuana veterans. Perhaps they were experimenting further. Billie Joe offers to take a friend who is down (someone he implies is the 'best thing in town') 'on a ride' to 'the other side' to cheer him up. Yet, the best thing in town probably refers to the best pot (or something stronger) in town. On 'Green Day', Billie Joe sang, 'Picture sounds of insects', and on this song, he sings, 'Eerie colors and all I see are sounds' and 'Faces of mysteries of the earth,' indicating his inebriated state. Here, the escapist Billie Joe is medicating with narcotics, whereas on 'Green Day' he was just experimenting.

Side B (listed as 'Ashtray'):

'Strangeland' (Lyrics: Armstrong; Music: Green Day)

In the speedy 'Strangeland,' we find a strangely-happy Billie Joe, but he warbles the words, since Mike and Al are driving so fast over the speed limit. His mumbling is a detriment to a nifty vocal melody. The chorus also is overly adrenalized as to partially mute its memorability. There are no band dynamics for most of the EP, except for Dirnt's warbled bass riff. What's lacking is the band's attention to the lyric. Armstrong is singing about calm, yet the band seems to blast away.

The song finds Billie Joe still living in a great mood, and the lyric is more-ambitious but lacks focus. He's trying to explain that – whether physically or mentally – existing in a calming, soothing space feels like a 'strangeland,' because he's usually sad or pessimistic, as just about every previous Green Day song has indicated. 'My eyes are clear and now I'm cured,' he sings enthusiastically. He's a hippie, content in his sanctuary – his almost hippie-like approach in lines about a 'love from mankind.'

'My Generation' (Pete Townshend)

The Who represent Green Day's first classic-rock wisdom shared with the masses. As Green Day's catalog grew, plenty of classic rock influences could be found in their originals, and occasionally they'd record a cover. The Who were a major influence on the band. Pete Townshend wrote the 1965 single 'My Generation,' which appeared on The Who's debut album *The Who Sings*

My Generation. The famous 1960s hit about the generation gap easily fits into the punk world, and no one batted an eye when Green Day used it to close the EP. It keeps the stop/start rhythm, and Al Sobrante and Mike sing the harmonies. The most memorable moment is when Armstrong screams during one of the breaks: 'Heineken? Fuck that shit!,' and we hear a bottle break like he threw it into the corner of the studio. The track ends with a silly but fittingly-sloppy party atmosphere with Armstrong's guitar solo and siren effect.

On 1 October 1991, Lookout! Records released the CD compilation *1039 Smoothed Out Slappy Hours*. In 2004 it was reissued in a deluxe edition, and again by Reprise Records in 2007. The compilation gathered Green Day's first 2 EPs *1000 Hours* and *Slappy,* and the debut album *39/Smooth*. The *39/ Smooth* tracks were placed first, followed by the two EPs, plus the additional closing track 'I Want To Be Alone' (from *The Big One*: a Flipside Records compilation released in 1991). The deluxe version added four tracks – 'Studio Banter', and 'One For The Razorbacks,' 'Paper Lanterns' and 'Words I Might Have Ate' live from WMMR.

'I Want To Be Alone' (Lyrics: Armstrong; Music: Green Day)

This weak track is one of the few occasions where almost everything fails. The arrangement is standard, as are the playing and singing. But it had all been done before and better. Armstrong adds a harmony to his main vocal track without using Mike. The guitar break is standard, but it's the best moment of a rare Green Day song that starts with a chorus.

Back in Billie Joe's bedroom, we again see our depressed singer striving for full isolation, to live in his misery. With all the problems of the first two EPs and the initial album, he's had enough, and doesn't care if the listeners he's addressing want to help him; they'll just be another burden.

Though the band's sound and lyrical themes were consistent over four releases, their chemistry was fluctuating. John Kiffmeyer wasn't quite meshing with the band like he did when they first formed, and Kiffmeyer was transferring to a different college and was losing interest in the band. In 2009, Billie Joe told Larry Livermore that John didn't tell the band he was leaving: 'And I was hurt. It blew me away. One, because I had to hear it from someone else, but also because, yeah, he was a big influence to us. We were so young, and he's a really smart person. We learned a lot from him. He was already a veteran of the scene, with Isocracy. He knew so much, and he worked really hard. But I think he's one of those guys who got really self-conscious about the kind of music we were playing.'

Green Day opened the fishing-tackle box and unloaded the hooks while singing of love, much more than typical punk rock bands did. If Billie Joe was correct, John, in a way, subconsciously considered Green Day to be a punk band and compared them to punk contemporaries. Meanwhile, Billie Joe and Mike didn't necessarily feel they were a punk band or a pop-punk band. They were just a rock band that played fast, hard music with plenty of appeal. Many would call it pop-punk, but trying to label Green Day just causes confusion and bitterness. As their fame grew, the 1990s' labelling sensitivity would touch them along with countless rock bands. Whether it was the label of 'sellout' or 'imitation wannabe punk' etc., Green Day and many other bands suffered many headaches over categorization.

By September, Tré Cool from Larry Livermore's Lookouts became Green Day's new and permanent drummer. A one-person party, Tré was such a fun personality and an amazing drummer. The combination was a major attraction to Billie Joe and Mike. It took a bit of time to find the chemistry, but they found it.

Frank Edwin Wright III was born on 9 December 1972 in Frankfurt, West Germany. Recently playing in The Lookouts, he'd briefly been part of Samiam (a Dr. Seuss reference). He grew up in Willits, California, living with his Vietnam War pilot father and older sister. Larry Livermore hired him for The Lookouts when Wright was only 12. He adopted the name Tré Cool, since he was *the third* Frank Wright. The word 'tres' means 'very' in French but sounds the same as the Spanish word 'tré.' Adding 'cool' – which means 'cool,' obviously – adds up to 'very cool' or 'Tré Cool'.

Kerplunk! (1991)

Personnel:
Billie Joe Armstrong: lead vocals, guitar; drums, backing vocals ('Dominated Love Slave')
Mike Dirnt: bass, backing vocals.
Tré Cool: drums; lead vocal, guitar ('Dominated Love Slave')
Producers: Andy Ernst, Green Day
Recorded at Art Of Ears studio, San Francisco, California
Label: Lookout!
Release date: 17 December 1991
Chart: US: -
CD and cassette versions added the Sweet Children EP.

Once the band worked out their new chemistry, they were set. The three have since been through it *all* together, entering their fourth decade in the 2020s as a team seemingly crazy-glued together for life. The band and everyone around them felt they were more explosive, powerful, dynamic and creative with Cool on the drums.

With their chemistry thriving and their songwriting improving, *Kerplunk* finds Green Day in their prime. It's one of their most beloved albums, serving as a shoulder to lean on for generations of teens struggling with anxiety over the present and future. Most of the songs were written in the first or second-person voice like much of their indie material, and a lot of it takes place in the present with plenty of thoughts about an uncertain future. With their sound still relatively lo-fi, *Kerplunk* qualifies as an all-time great lo-fi indie-rock record. It is considered the template and foundation for Green Day's 1990s sound, and their overall signature sound.
Any cover song they did live, usually had a pop-punk arrangement, and when Green Day pops up on radio, their sound is instantly identifiable.

Sadly, for producer Andy Ernst, it was his final recording with Green Day. They entered Art of Ears and worked on the album sporadically from May to September 1991. The resulting four-million-selling *Kerplunk* is considered one of indie rock's greatest albums – one that helped more than one generation of youth deal with their teen years. Though the majority of the album's sales occurred after the band's 1994 album *Dookie*, through the 2010s, teenagers were writing comments on YouTube *Kerplunk* videos about Green Day positively impacting their lives.

'2000 Light Years Away' (Armstrong, Dirnt, Cool, Jesse Michaels, Pete Rypins (listed as Rippins), Dave 'E.C.' Henwood)

This is is the song title you whisper to the bouncer when you want to get into the Green Day indie fan club. It's their most popular Lookout release, a fan favorite, and a band favorite since it continues to be in setlists years later. It's about long-distance love, since Billie Joe lived in California, and his future wife Adrienne lived in Minnesota. This stellar heart-pumper initiates the band's growth by highlighting their new drummer. The splendid construction of the songwriting and arranging are expert steps up from earlier material. Listen to how the band politely drops out, leaving Mike to pluck away on bass dreamily as Armstrong gathers his thoughts aloud. Then, the power trio ferociously leap back into the amazing chorus, emphasized by Mike's added harmonies.

It's a romantic love song, set – guess where? – in Billie Joe's bedroom. 'I sit alone in my bedroom, staring at the wall/I've been up all damn night long.' His insomniac tendencies grab hold of him, and he is infatuated with a woman – but with an optimistic twist: this one actually likes him! The title appears to be a nod to The Rolling Stones' 1967 song '2000 Light Years From Home.' He 'holds his breath' in anticipation for their next meeting, and during the chorus, he knows she's holding his 'malachite so tight.'

Green Day – the punk band not afraid of love and romance – appeared for an hour on radio station KROQ's 'Lovelines' program in early 1994, helping the celebrity Dr. Drew solve callers' relationship issues. One caller asked about the malachite line. Billie Joe answered, 'It's a stone, it's a green stone and I gave it to someone once. I gave someone a malachite and they live 2000 miles away.' In 2020, he remembered the background for *Rolling Stone*:

The first tour that Green Day ever went on, I met my wife Adrienne at a house party in Minneapolis. She asked for an address, because we had run out of our vinyl. Then we started corresponding and kind of became pen pals, and having these long talks, running up phone bills. Then Green Day booked this mini-tour. We drove from California all the way out to Minnesota. Nobody really knew why we were driving all the way to Wisconsin and Minnesota to just play, like, four shows, but I was really just going back to see her. On the way back, I wrote '2000 Light Years Away.' The song just wrote itself. I put it down on an acoustic guitar and sent her a cassette of it. It's been a staple in our set ever since, and it led into many, many, many songs I've been writing about her for the next almost-30 years.

'One For The Razorbacks' (Lyrics: Armstrong; Music: Green Day)

This muscular and metallic track is padded with a football-like title and more melody and hooks. The band score another touchdown in both departments as they run over the competition on their way to the end zone. Armstrong performs one of his final guitar solos of the decade, and Mike sings the final line of all the verses, and with Billie Joe on the choruses.

'Well, look in this direction/I know it's not perfection/But I will try to bring you up again now' continues to show how the lyrical themes are aligned with the then-fresh genres of emo and shoegaze. A lot of Billie Joe's lyrics in this era unveil a humble romantic. 'I know I am crazy and a bit lazy,' he continues, acknowledging another personal mental flaw when pining for a woman.

It's still unclear why the title includes 'razorbacks' – the type of pig that represents the century-old nickname for the University of Arkansas' sports teams. Perhaps Billie Joe meant the protagonist was a pig searching for scraps to feast on, symbolizing his greed in trying to satisfy his needs by seeking a vulnerable woman and acting as if he's only there to help.

'Welcome To Paradise' (Lyrics: Armstrong; Music: Green Day)
This marvelous song is a catalog highlight, and the band's first major leap musically and lyrically. They knew they had a special song on their hands, and later re-recorded it for their major-label debut *Dookie*. (Because of that version's hit qualities and popularity, its background and details will be fleshed out under that entry.)

On *Kerplunk,* the track's major-label production and powerful sound is missing, but Mike Dirnt's first excellent bass line is firmly in place.

'Christie Road' (Lyrics: Armstrong; Music: Green Day)
The crunching grunge-like 'Christie Road' is another glorious melody and hook rolled between slices of metal and jangle. Spread on the lazy, hazy double-tracked Armstrong vocals, and you have a winning sandwich. The dynamics kick-up as Billie Joe presents an anti-guitar solo break that leads into a dramatic buildup. The solid bridge withstands the waves of metallic punk. At one point, Armstrong's squeal is the single strand keeping the song going.

The song is about a thoroughfare in Martinez, California, that runs alongside railroad tracks. Like 'Strangeland' – which was about finding a peaceful escape in the world (probably) through drug use – 'Christie Road' is about the peace found in an isolated location. 'Give me something to do to kill some time' and 'Gotta get away or my brains will explode' continue themes that match well with grunge and the band's later material on *Dookie*, *Insomniac* and *Nimrod*. Billie Joe's then-girlfriend Erica Paleno explained this personal sanctuary to author Marc Spitz:

I would steal his notebooks, his lyric book. I still have them, but they're tucked away. There's the original version of 'Christie Road', which he wrote for my mom and me. It's about meeting him at the train tracks and sneaking out of the house, because my mom didn't let me. I was always grounded. We thought it was so broad-based and open-minded for people who were outsiders, like us.

'Private Ale' (Lyrics: Armstrong; Music: Green Day)
'Hello, I'm here!,' Billie Joe blurts out over a typically-lively band on the solid pop-punk 'Private Ale,' continuing the fast-paced routes Green Day like to take. They roll with sonic urgency through most of *Kerplunk*, but they veer off the highway into a jangly, bass-heavy ditch where a drunk guy lives. An

odd deep voice mumbles complaints on the instrumental break. The band then get their car back on its wheels and onto the highway once more. The melody and chorus are reliably satisfying.

Billie Joe sings, 'Think of my future/I don't know now,' which harkens back to '409 In Your Coffeemaker' and Operation Ivy's 'Knowledge'. He feels forced to choose, ahead of naturally finding his place in the world. 'Private Ale' combines his thoughts on the future and pining for an unavailable woman.

'Dominated Love Slave' (Lyrics: Cool; Music: Green Day)
This early fan favorite is a mock-country hoedown with Billie Joe on drums and Tré on guitar. Live, the crowd and band could have a few laughs. The cowboys gather on the humorous break and awkwardly end the song before the joke goes on too long.

This kinky lyric is Tré's first, and it displays his endlessly-youthful sense of humor. He wants to be the 'sex slave' of a dominatrix, and vividly describes the scene. He even mentions a belt sander that's used to smooth wooden surfaces. He requests staples, chains, and to be thrown into a pickup truck. The lighthearted debacle ends with a drunken harmony that perfectly caps off a night at the dude ranch.

'One Of My Lies' (Lyrics: Armstrong; Music: Green Day)
After a brief humorous aside, the band storm back with another priceless hook that's so catchy, it could serve fish dinners for a week. This is pop punk at its best, and though Green Day still don't identify with the genre, they play it to perfection. Dirnt is fantastic, and Tré lays low until the glorious chorus.

Much of the punk rock world sang about liars and those that deceive others to gain an advantage, but 'One Of My Lies' speaks to Green Day's more personal reflections. Billie Joe is back in his innocent past, where he felt like a child who would live forever. But maturity brings a better understanding of life and death, and Billie Joe tackles the subject by taking the escape route out of a theme still too heavy for him to fully contemplate. He touches on religion concerning a possible afterlife, but without scientific proof, he's skeptical thinking life ends when the physical body dies. It's not an anti-religious song, but more about a teenager who needs time to figure it out.

'80' (Lyrics: Armstrong; Music: Green Day)
The sensational '80' continues the terrific songwriting, and the band light up the sky with fantastic rays of tough-shelled pop punk. The amazing chorus is perhaps the best on *Kerplunk* – easily singable, and blessed with an ace Dirnt harmony. '80' is an exceptional effort.

Adie was a nickname Billie Joe used for his future wife Adrienne Nesser, and the nickname's sound is close enough to '80' to suggest this song was a secret message to her. Tortured by the '2000 light years' of distance between them at the time, Billie Joe goes the personal route, explaining how the separation is eroding his mental state. He's on the edge of insanity, and really ramps up his wretched mental condition, opening the song with 'My mental stability reaches its bitter end,' and calls love a 'disease.'

'80' showcases the theme of the mind affecting the body as a result of worry and loneliness. He feels like he should be locked in a padded room, so he doesn't try to bang some sense into his head. He's been drinking heavily to dull the pain, but no one wants to help a 'drunken fool.' By the end, he twists the tune by declaring his love of this torture, because he'd rather be tortured by temptation than have no one who cares about him. Billie Joe wasn't kidding about loving Adie – he's still married to her almost three decades later.

'Android' (Lyrics: Armstrong; Music: Green Day)

The adrenaline-filled 'Android' finds us wrapped in grinding metallic guitar distortion, lots of Tré hi-hat, and a Mike bass that fittingly locks into Armstrong's part. There's not much to the band's effort – typically energetic. But on the break, the yammering drunk guy from 'Private Ale' is back and now flushing a toilet. The band must've been exploring the studio, finding several sound effects. The post-chorus guitar riff sounds like a sped-up version of the melody from the Nirvana song 'Sliver.'. With a sped-up vocal harmony, Dirnt sounds like an alien.

The term 'android' usually ties in with technology and cell phones, but back in the 1990s, it was only used when referring to a human-looking robot. The term doubled personally for Green Day, as it was one of their nicknames for producer Andy Ernst, who was also billed as 'Andro' previously. In 2011, Billie Joe tweeted, ''Android' was about a homeless man walking down College Avenue. I was drinking coffee with Tré.'

Verse one profiles the homeless man, who's wearing ladies shoes. Then the chorus finds Billie Joe wondering, if he fails at his musical career, will he wind up homeless and looking 'crazy.' Verse two compares the homeless man's past in school to Billie Joe's present situation. Armstrong had just dropped out of high school, and asks if the homeless man was like him when he was in school. 'Did he hide his hopes behind a smile and smoking dope?' Ever personal on song bridges, Armstrong wonders if it's worth singing about his 'chemical emotions' on all these songs if nobody buys their music.

'No One Knows' (Lyrics: Armstrong; Music: Green Day)

After a brief solo-bass opening initiates a lazy pace, the weighty, metallic chugging covers the remainder of this lethargically-mid-tempo track. Dirnt's bass expertly underscores Armstrong's guitar. The vocal melody has led on most tunes, whereas on their next album, Dirnt was to lead the melody with his excellent bass lines. Tré will also see better days, as he's just trying to fit into the band's chemistry, choosing toms as a primary weapon here. The song has a little counter-moment where Armstrong overdubs different words in a second vocal that overlaps with the basic track: a trick they wouldn't continue.

Billie Joe appears to be questioning authority on this song about having fun when you're young before adult responsibilities become the priority. Like most youth, Billie Joe is addressing either teachers or parents – usually, the stems of authority dismayed in seeing a young person's struggle with growing up. He wonders if his antagonist is purposely scheming to make him feel guilty about partying, by telling him he won't ever be anything as an adult. His defensive response is that no one can predict the future.

'Who Wrote Holden Caulfield?'(Lyrics: Armstrong; Music: Green Day)

This top-rated song switches between speed-metal verses and the band's typical pop-punk for the catchy chorus. Dirnt joins in on the mic, and significantly strengthens the refrain. The break provides dynamic excitement, and the stop/start rhythm bolstering the choruses has an impact on the ears by upping the memorability.

Holden Caulfield (since Billie Joe is asking) is the main character and narrative voice of J. D. Salinger's famous novel *Catcher in the Rye.* In the 1990s, it was a book tied to practically every high school curriculum in the country. Billie Joe explained to *Spin:* 'It's a classic from the '50s. My teachers forced me to read it in school, so naturally, I didn't. I did finally read it later, and, ironically, rebellion is kind of what it's about. This guy tries to fit in, but can never quite do it. Finally, he just celebrates his uniqueness by rebelling and getting kicked out of high school and going on this crazy adventure. I can identify with that.'

In 2020, Armstrong remembered the song in *Rolling Stone*: 'It's a song about forgetting what you're going to say ... It's trying to get motivated to do something because your elders tell you you have to get motivated. So then you get frustrated and you think that you should do something, but you end up doing nothing. But then you enjoy it.'

'Who Wrote Holden Caulfield?' is Billie Joe's favorite song on *Kerplunk,* according to his offhand comment found on their live album *Awesome As F**k.* The motivation theme was to continue on their later single, 'Longview.'

'Words I Might Have Ate' (Lyrics: Armstrong; Music: Green Day)

This poppy song is the first time we hear the band using acoustic guitar. Billie Joe contemplates more of his mistakes. It's almost as if he was calmed by finally reaching his goal of attaining a woman – so the sound is finally softer, losing any power or aggression. Like other Green Day songs, the melody helps tremendously. Even the 'why?' coda is catchy the way Armstrong delivers in different ways before the (rare) fade-out.

For two albums and three EPs, our love-hungry protagonist has craved girls so badly he's gone crazy many times, holed up in his bedroom, reflecting on everything he did wrong. By the end of *Kerplunk*, he's finally gotten into a relationship. But by the time he meets up with his listeners to tell us he's happy, he's messed it all up and it may already be over:

> The love I bitched about, I finally found
> But now it's gone and I take the blame
> Now there's nothing left to do but take the pain
> Why?

As the chorus, the 'why's add up, because he doesn't know what he said that offended her. Well, happily for Armstrong, his life had grown away from the kid who couldn't get a date. He had been dating girls like Erica Palerno (the inspiration for 'Christie Road'), and Adrienne Nesser had also taken an interest in him by the time *Kerplunk* was issued.

Dookie (1994)

Personnel:
Billie Joe Armstrong: lead vocals, guitar; percussion ('All By Myself')
Mike Dirnt: bass, backing vocals
Tré Cool: drums; lead vocals, guitar ('All By Myself')
Producers: Rob Cavallo, Green Day
Recorded at Fantasy Records, Berkeley, California
Label: Reprise
Release date: 1 February 1994
Charts: US: 2, UK: 13
Singles: 'Longview,' 'Welcome To Paradise,' 'Basket Case,' 'When I Come Around,' 'She'

Dookie is the best-selling punk album of all time. The fact should be considered a tremendous accomplishment. But to the indie crowd at Gilman, Green Day signing with major label Warner Bros. Records meant they were sellouts. It didn't matter that they were still using their signature sound, which sounded better than ever with high-quality production and a better studio. The indie crowd iced Green Day out of the scene and banned them. The band took it hard, but eventually, they'd have 20 million new friends as fans to cheer them on. The Green Day legacy would've endured had they stopped after *Dookie*. It has fantastic songwriting, excellent performances and a winning charisma and group personality that was evident in the music, videos and their live shows.

Green Day had to trade in their indie credentials to accomplish their goal of greater reach, resulting in a vicious Gilman club backlash. Signing to Warner Bros. subsidiary Reprise Records wasn't just a help financially and with distribution, but it brought new sonic powers that resulted in a fantastic in-your-face sound that freshened and sharpened their stellar songwriting. Producer Rob Cavallo was signed on after smoking pot and jamming with the band upon first meeting them. He was to remain their primary producer for decades, with an occasional exception. Cavallo and the band learning about the recording studio, drastically increased their potency, emphasized their hooks and opened them up to being more ambitious. Mike Dirnt became one of rock's most popular bassists since he got many solo moments and thoroughly thrived in the spotlight.

Dookie isn't quite as personal to the band as their earlier material was, since Armstrong's life was looking up while the album was looking down. The LP is as much of a downer as found in the grunge world at the time. Many of the songs are a contrast with Green Day's reality, and the album ties in so well with grunge that fans who were tired of that genre could reach for something poppier and peppier but with teen-angst lyrics that Gen X could relate to. The lyrics were universal enough to also inspire upcoming generations. Billie Joe took on the role of teen-angst spokesman throughout the album, shifting from the thoughts of women that occupied most of their indie material, to a head-on look at growing up into an adult. For the band's youthful fan base, they were figuring out the trials and tribulations a teen may face as they grow and learn that life isn't all candy and toys. Green Day may have been self-deprecating, self-deflating and self-defacing like grunge, but it was without the anger and feelings of retribution and revenge against the rest of the world.

Dookie ended Green Day's innocent-nice-guy status. Sex, drugs and violence are finally all in the queue to be discussed. Attacks on old acquaintances, Billie Joe's stepfather and general society find their way onto the album, mixed with coming-of-age songs. *Dookie* is one of the most influential 1990s punk records. It had five hit singles and ultimately sold 20,000,000 copies.

'Burnout' (Lyrics: Armstrong; Music: Green Day)

The bleak and distraught 'Burnout' burns fiery with a new and improved rhythm section. It's still Mike and Tré, but my goodness, have they improved. Here they blast through an excellent rocker that holds their most powerful break yet. The sound is so in-your-face and aggressive – when Tré takes his first drum fills in the stop/start section, it's clear the band have just rocked harder than they ever have before. The terrific melody and hooks continue.

Though the band have shifted to a wider what-do-I-do-with-my-life-in-the-future theme, *Dookie* opens its doors to find our narrator in his comfortable safe haven: his bedroom. 'I'm burning up and out and growing bored/In my smoked-out boring room.' Reeking of green days, his bedroom had seen a fog in the *Kerplunk* closer 'Words I Might Have Ate.' In 'Burnout,' he hasn't had a haircut, he's bored with his room, has apathy for his life's goals thinking he has no chance to secure them anyway, and he's too embarrassed to reveal his depressing feelings, singing, 'I'll live inside this mental cave/Throw my emotions in the grave.' His apathy causes him to go out at night and step in line to 'walk amongst the dead,' as if them having typical jobs meant they were zombies hanging around at night only to go to work in the day and do as their told. It continues the individualist theme that a person will burn out because they'll grow tired of living life by others' wishes. These are the main motivations of the characters we'll discover in *American Idiot* and *21st Century Breakdown*.

'Having A Blast' (Lyrics: Armstrong; Music: Green Day)

This gloriously-delusional madman-fest is fantastic. Melody and hooks are a staple in just about every *Dookie* moment, but each tune has its own set of exploding dynamics, and this is no exception. It speeds along normally, with Dirnt helping on chorus harmonies. But another stop/start moment for the bridge finds this band has been in the gym working out – everything hits harder, like a heavyweight boxer.

The frustration of 'Burnout' (and almost every song in the catalog so far) has finally driven our narrator over the edge. This was the boiling point – or, for this tune, the bombing point. The album cover may have been comical, just like the title 'Having A Blast' is sardonic. Yet, the melodramatic song itself has little humor. It's perhaps Green Day's most vehemently dark and violent track. They sing as a suicide bomber is about to blow himself up with everybody else, because he's sick of himself and the world.

The '1000 Hours' romantic kiss under the starlit night has morphed into something more deadly. Armstrong asks us in the second person to 'close your eyes and kiss yourself goodbye': the worst kind of kiss. A woman put him in pain, so he's seeking his revenge. There's no conclusion to the confusion, just citing the violent motivation with no story arc, like later songs in their career. In 2011, Billie Joe tweeted: 'I wrote 'Having A Blast' in Cleveland in 1992. Had a great show at the Euclid, but the rest of the night was miserable.'

'Chump' (Lyrics: Armstrong; Music: Green Day)

'Chump' is always known for being the song linked to the more popular 'Longview' But it still has the perfected Green Day formula of a fast rhythm with exciting drum fills and melodic bass sometimes leading the song, grungy distorted guitar and Billie Joe's snotty nasal vocals.

Well, the album didn't end after two songs. It's safe to say the lethal blast of 'Having A Blast' never happened. But that doesn't mean the anger has totally subsided. 'Chump' is another attack song for the protagonist's ex-girlfriend's new boyfriend. Like he will on 'Basket Case,' Billie Joe gives us a multiple-choice question for the chorus since he's undecidedly unconfident about his mental state. 'Maybe it's just jealousy, or maybe I'm just dumb' is the line he opens and closes the chorus with. He calls his adversary 'magic man' and 'egocentric plasticman.' Billie Joe has indicated 'Chump' is based on a friend named Amanda whom he greatly respected. But after dating Billie Joe, she left him.

Halfway through, the song cuts, and as Armstrong's guitar-distortion squeals fade, we're left with Dirnt plucking away hard on a long bass break. It's intercut with Pete Townshend winding-arm guitar power chords until Billie Joe can't wait any longer and blasts out flurries of notes that cause a calamity-constructed confusion. The song winds down, leaving Mike to let his bass part gradually transform into his famous 'Longview' riff. it's one of the band's new dynamics of letting the song ride on the bass alone. As Dirnt continues, the band start a new song without him batting an eye or removing a finger from the strings. Fortunately, it's Mike's most famous bass line ever.

'Longview' (Lyrics: Armstrong; Music: Green Day)

The exciting 'Chump' coda winds down, leaving Mike on bass to continue the performance through the transition into Green Day's breakthrough hit single 'Longview.' He claims he'd taken LSD prior to thinking up the famous and brilliant bass line. It bounds down the street to meet its friend: Billie Joe's deliberately weary vocal. But the narrator awakens with an amazing vocal hook for the thunderous chorus that plows through the fields of woe. Its low/loud verse/chorus dynamic, punkish attitude, metal riffage and aggravated lyric were some of the track's elements that overlapped post-grunge. We're hanging out in the living room for a change, and as a bonus, we could see it on television as Green Day played out the lyric in their first music video. In both the audio and video, he's trapped in his mental prison. Billie Joe told *Billboard*:

> I really loved the song by The Pretenders called 'Message Of Love,' and wanted to write a song like that, but we needed a bass line. Mike is sitting on the floor in the kitchen tripping balls, and he had his bass on, and he goes, 'I figured it out, man! I figured it out.' He played the bass line for me for the first time right there. Then we ended up playing it the next day, and it just stuck. The lyrics to it are about feeling like a loser, watching television, jerking off and feeling lonely. I was pretty frightened at the time. I was in limbo. I didn't have a girlfriend – it took like four years for me and Adrienne to get together, from like '90 until '94.

After driving down drug roads, smoking his inspiration and 'tripping away to paradise,' Armstrong has rounded the circle of boredom. In verse three, he mentions his mother, who advises him to get a summer job, but 'She don't like the one she's got.' His mom worked as a waitress to support Billie Joe and his siblings. He told Larry Livermore about her in a 2009 interview: 'I rarely saw my mom, because she was working graveyard shifts at a 24-hour diner. It was hard on her, but she had to do it. There's one thing I have to say about my mom: that she's a survivor.'

'Welcome To Paradise' (Re-recorded) (Lyrics: Armstrong; Music: Green Day)
'Welcome To Paradise' take two, aaannd… action! Though not much has changed since its Lookout crib days, the grown-up 'Welcome To Paradise' proves how much better, more lively and colossal Green Day's sound had become on Reprise with the help of producer Rob Cavallo. The chorus is at its best when the band pause to allow space for Tré's fantastically-powerful drum fills. Billie Joe lunges into the percussion madness, spewing out the title as he plays one of his greatest guitar riffs. The gutsy, adventurous instrumental break sees the band fully free to wreak havoc with reckless youth rebellion and abandon. Mike sticks hard to his chattering bass line, and slowly Tré and Billie Joe sneak up from behind as they seamlessly blend back in with a stellar, choppy rhythm like they're cutting up a meat loaf for dinner.

Tré is used sparingly, but then works up an odder rhythm, and Armstrong visits the East, whipping up a very rare eastern-influenced guitar part bringing an exotic feel to this paradise. Then he gradually climbs his way back up into the song's typical pop-punk meat. Tré is working on a higher plane than most drummers, building up each chorus like he's instilling confidence in Armstrong to let loose.

Billie Joe is done living at home, and needs a change of scenery to spark his dull life. He thinks the world is his oyster when he sets off to conquer it, but instead finds the darker side of life. It's the MTV generation's 'Like A Rolling Stone.' Bob Dylan was an influence on Green Day, and in 2009 they released a cover version of the song.

'Welcome To Paradise' was a turning point in the frustrated romantic – partially based on Billie Joe – that serves as the protagonist. In real life, Billy Joe was set to marry Adrienne in the summer, and had already left his mother's *crib*, staying at friends' houses often. The turning point was more about Billie Joe's growth as a lyricist.

The first lines, 'Mother can you hear me whining/It's been three whole weeks since I left your home,' reveals we're reading a distressing letter the singer wrote to his mother, serving as a new frame for a previously-visited subject, growing up. He's bitten off more than he can chew, and he's asking for a lifeline. He adds the word 'whole' as if they felt like the longest three weeks of his life. He lives in the 'slums,' with cracked streets, broken homes both physically and domestically, the mentally unstable homeless, and bullets flying. It's his terror, his daymare and nightmare. But by verse two, Armstrong has grown accustomed to his environment through the habit of waking up there every day, though the 'wasteland' is still the same wreck.

Once the guitar break passes, so have six months, and for verse three, he cleverly alters the first and second verses. He replaces lyrics and adds new ones to the first verse, that advances the story six months ahead. 'Whining' becomes 'laughing,' 'three weeks' becomes 'six months,' and now he's happy there. It's a universal thread that many can relate to, and because of the stellar music and hooks, it became a 1990s anthem, living on, touching further generations. Billie Joe spoke to *Rolling Stone* in 2020:

I had moved out of my house in the suburbs, to West Oakland, into a warehouse that was rat-infested and in a really fucked-up neighborhood, with a lot of crazy punks and friends. I was paying $50 a month for rent, which was great, because, being in a band, you got paid a couple hundred bucks here and there, so it was easy to pay for rent, eat Top Ramen and buy weed. It was an eye-opening experience. Suddenly I was on my own, smack out in one of the gnarliest neighborhoods in Oakland. You look around and you see cracked streets and broken homes and ghetto neighborhoods, and you're in the middle of it. You're scared, thinking, 'How do I get out of here?' Then, suddenly it starts to feel like home. There is a sort of empathy that you have for your surroundings when you're around junkies and homelessness and gang warfare. 'A gunshot rings out at the station/Another urchin snaps and left dead on his own' – I was describing exactly what my surroundings were. There's not a part of that song that isn't true. It's a great live song to crank into. I think the musicality of the (bridge) is a foreshadowing of what things were to come for us in the future, whether we knew it or not.

'Pulling Teeth' (Lyrics: Armstrong; Music: Green Day)
This jolly melodic tune sounds like a walk in the park, but it's more like a trip to the dentist. The melody is a bright shining white smile as Armstrong sings like he's still in love with this violent woman. Mike plays serious-minded deep bass, and Tré holds back the aggression. The melodic bridge is the best moment of this lower-profile *Dookie* track.

Supposedly, 'Pulling Teeth' was inspired by a fight Mike Dirnt had with his girlfriend. It has an overexaggerated physically painful melodrama, sung facetiously to indicate the protagonist's mental scars over a rocky relationship. It reminds some of the mock-hoedown 'Dominated Love Slave.' The band chose this lyrical avenue of physical pain representing mental anguish, as one to focus on further with their follow-up album *Insomniac*.

'Basket Case' (Lyrics: Armstrong; Music: Green Day)
When the second *Dookie* hit 'Basket Case' opens, it's just a chugging punk guitar and Armstrong telling the story of his insanity plea. The band make room for the godsend of a melody and incredible chorus: one of the best in 1990s rock. Billie Joe fully performs both verse and chorus solo, prior to the band's slamming breakthrough. The top-notch performance triggers all the right brain cells; it's so well-written. Tré's chaotic drum fills add to the confusion and loud voices in Billie Joe's head. The band fire on all cylinders, to provide this memorably sparkling effort.

If 'Longview' was the crazed culmination of all the frustration and boredom of leading a lonely life, 'Basket Case' was the culmination of Billie Joe asking himself if he was crazy at least a dozen times previously. The mental health theme had been used countless times, but here he fully focuses on the subject, and his lyric writing is drastically improved. He asks a question right off the bat – 'Do you have the time to listen to me whine about nothing and everything all at once?' – just like he began 'Welcome To Paradise' with 'Dear mother, can you hear me whining?' It's very polite of him to ask if he can whine before doing it anyway. He told *Vulture* in 2021:

I never expected 'Basket Case' to be a single. I think I would've probably chosen 'Burnout' or 'She' – something like that. Thank God I got outvoted for that single. This keeps coming to mind. After *Dookie* came out, I think when Basket Case started to get really big, a friend of mine's band went to a truck stop, and they found a Green Day air freshener for their car. This is something that wasn't a part of our merchandise at all. It was just this bootleg freshener. And that moment really sticks out for me.

Armstrong continues to psychoanalyze his protagonist's inner feelings like a chatterbox therapist constantly breaking doctor/client privacy privileges. The singer clearly has many issues in his life, though he doesn't think anyone cares. He admits he's melodramatic directly after 'Having A Blast' and 'Welcome To Paradise': a couple of Green Day's most melodramatic songs. He's neurotic and paranoid, like in 'Chump'; he gives himself 'the creeps,' like in 'Burnout' and 'Having a Blast,' and he's stoned, like in 'Longview.' The list of neuroses in the first verse and chorus, direct him to a therapist.

Verse two deals with his visit, where the therapist tells him he's not getting enough sex. He follows her advice and finds a male prostitute, who he refers to as 'she'. She is instantly bored with him and grows tired of his whining. It's a colorful verse, that mocks how society handles mental health within the self-effacing and self-aware commentary that he's such a whiner – even a prostitute who's simply there for the money, can't properly do their job.

It could've been a seriously-depressing song, but the band's youthful, extroverted personalities create a more dynamic, multi-faceted lyric. The balance carried this song a long way.

'She' (Lyrics: Armstrong; Music: Green Day)

Like on 'Longview,' it's Mike Dirnt who leads off another fantastic pop-punk rocker: the big hit 'She.' As Armstrong introduces us to his latest crush, Dirnt finds an almost beautiful bass motif: one of his finest performances.

'She' is one of Billie Joe Armstrong's favorites, and is a successful hit single and a fan favorite. With him playing the surprisingly-efficient therapist, he diagnoses her as a healthy individual who is not the problem. However, she is letting society control her, so she should live her life the way she wants and filter out the noise of those that oppose her, as Armstrong's great lyric can attest to.

'A sullen riot penetrating through her mind' is one of Billie Joe's best lines, because it illuminates the Riot grrrl era and women who were striving for more female voices in music and in general. Riot grrrls would form bands, create fanzines and hold meetings discussing women's rights, but through a punk-attitude lens. Armstrong wrote the song for Amanda: a Cal student who'd shared the same beliefs as riot grrrls. Armstrong told *Rolling Stone* in 2014:

I will play 'She' for the rest of my life. It has aged well with me. I had a girlfriend named Amanda, this Cal student. I learned a lot about feminism through her. She gave me an education that I think was very timely for me. I was just a dumb kid, high-school dropout. She was telling me about the way women have been objectified for so many years, and I was just listening. I wrote this as a love song to her, but it was also about learning about her activism. When it says 'Scream at me until my ears bleed,' I was kind of going, 'I'm here to listen.' With any kind of activism, the first thing you need to do is be a good listener. The song becomes about an understanding. I'm really proud of it. It's very stripped-down and simple, with three chords. It's kind of a cult hero. Those are the special kinds of songs.

'Wait... ing for a sign to smash the silence with the brick of self-control' is another stellar line – the imagery and the violent action of breaking through her own walls of solitude that hide her from societal negativity that she can no longer face, and the manipulation of the term 'self-control' from holding back from personal bad habits to a literal definition of she being the person in control of her own life. Note how Billie waits after he sings 'wait.' 'Are you locked up in a world that's being planned out for you?' reminds us of Billie Joe's unsettled high school dropout thoughts in earlier songs like '409 In Your Coffeemaker,' 'Knowledge,' 'Android,' 'Who Wrote Holden Caufield?' and 'No One Knows.' From the earlier personal experience of having doubts over his future years, he's able to help Amanda find herself, despite the world telling her what she should be.

'Sassafras Roots' (Lyrics: Armstrong; Music: Green Day)
As a very simple song with a lot of 'wasting your time' vocal repetitions included to perhaps purposely waste a listener's time with the same line over and over, 'Sassafras Roots' is basically about two people who aren't dating, so why not date each other? The band also keeps things fairly light, and Dirnt issues a fun, melodically-snazzy bass line. It's a boring guy with a band who tries to be boring, yet they fail miserably. Green Day are too exciting, energetic, lively and potent to be boring. The lighthearted sentiment is the most casual crush a Green Day song protagonist has had, and it alleviates the tension of other songs. Mike named the song after the genus of a deciduous tree – the root in root beer – perhaps thinking the song's two bored characters are as boring as root beer compared to beer, but it's unclear. In 2012, Billie Joe tweeted: "She' is about a girl named Amanda. So is 'Sassafras Roots' and so is 'Whatsername'. Ooh... that's a good factoid.'

'When I Come Around' (Lyrics: Armstrong; Music: Green Day)
The band's second major post-grunge hit (and fourth single) sounds nothing like punk with its metallic riff: the album's best riff. The band's crunching militant rhythm (a bit like the stiffer 'Christie Road') and Billie Joe's mammoth verse and chorus hooks feel larger than life thanks to Rob Cavallo's production. Though it's the most riff-based track, if there was to be one riff on *Dookie* fleshed out, let it be this riff. "Cause you know where I can be found' is accented by Tré's drum fills, creating a brief tension representing the waiting woman. Then Armstrong sings the title, and the tension is relieved with his reassurance and the band's magnificent riff coming back around. Dirnt plays all around the main motif to keep the song flexible.

This is the first song to seriously get into the heart of a Green Day protagonist's relationship, but still maintain the *born-loser* identity that couldn't get a girl in the first place. Yet, despite maintaining his affinity for revealing his personal weaknesses, the voice comes from that of a more confident, experienced lover. He also references the protagonist's girlfriend as the one with the problems, like on 'She' and 'Sassafras Roots.' She's 'sitting around feeling sorry' for herself, lonely and crying. He claims he just needs some time on his own, away from her, but he is serious about the relationship. He tells her not to be uptight, and to not chase him around like a clingy girlfriend – just wait for him, and he'll be around. He admits that it's wrong of him to make her wait, since he's a 'loser' and a 'user' of the past with other women and that he doesn't want to feel the guilt of her not living life and having fun without him. He encourages her to leave if she needs to, in case she feels the relationship is forced, but ultimately would like her to be patient and he'll come around, not just physically but figuratively. Eventually, he'll be ready to go steady.

'Coming Clean' (Lyrics: Armstrong; Music: Green Day)

Armstrong bursts through the door alone, announcing that he's a confused teen. Then the band bowl him over as they rush through the door into the confession room, and rock out, shaking the foundation. Another straight break is just what the grunge doctor ordered. There's lots of hi-hat from Tré between drum fills, and Dirnt churns up another stellar bass riff.

'Coming Clean' is a perfect example of Green Day's songwriting realities lagging behind Billie Joe's personal realities. Though Billie Joe was 21 at the time, the protagonist he plays is only 17, as heard in the opening line about being confused. Though many have linked this song to his comments about being bisexual, the song never alludes to a specific issue but serves as an umbrella for all teen issues.

Because of the ambiguity, 'Coming Clean' was instantly relatable for most teen Green Day fans, regardless of personal scenarios. The opening couplet '17 and strung-out on confusion/Trapped inside a role of disillusion' shows continuing lyrical depth by altering a phrase definition, this time using the term 'strung out' not to relay a drug message but to acknowledge that he's wasted from confusion over his blurred future. On Green Day's next tour, they used the gay band Pansy Division as their opening act. Billie Joe told *Rolling Stone* in 1994:

More personal politics. It is a little more about getting used to yourself or changing yourself or coming to grips with yourself, like the song 'Coming Clean.' Kids will always stop to think about the fact of the possibilities of not knowing what their sexuality is all about – Am I homosexual? Am I bisexual? Am I heterosexual? Am I no sexual? Or am I just plain sexual? People don't know what the fuck they are. I still struggle with that too – it's part of adolescence and growing up.

'Emenius Sleepus' (Dirnt)

Another song with no intro – just the guitar riff that powers the track – the skillful 'Emenius Sleepus' continues the pop-punk winning streak, Armstrong laying out long slabs of chorded distortion. On the break, Tré breaks out a manic fill from his locker, dusts it off and rocks it out for a cool dynamic moment. While most bands would've been in filler territory, 'Enimus Sleepus' is relatively weak compared to the other songs here, but it's way above average, especially considering what the 'little kid' bass-heavy break adds.

This is one of Green Day's oddest song titles, so to decode it, a Latin lesson is required. 'Emenius Sleepus' means 'Sleep with the buyer,' though it looks more like 'Sleep with the enemy.' It's a quick and simple attack song written by Mike Dirnt. Mike's protagonist reunites with an old acquaintance who hasn't matured like himself. He's a spoiled person who's lost the kindness he used to display as a child. Mike continuously has Billie Joe sing that he wants to go home cause he's sick of the guy.

'In The End' (Lyrics: Armstrong; Music: Green Day)

There's just no time for intros and barely any time for outros as the band squeeze in a few final tracks. In this hardcore pop-punk track, Tré gets his listeners off on more speed-demon drum fills. Mike brings another memorable bass break, though this one's simpler and more rhythm-oriented than his typical melodic playing. It's the swiftest track here, and Tré gets a full week's fitness workout in less than two minutes: particularly in the *speed-core* break.

The lyric bombs continue with 'In The End' – a song similar to 'Chump' where Armstrong goes after a guy that's dating a woman Armstrong likes. In verse one, he gives us the visual of a jock misogynist. He sees right through the façade as heard in the chorus, before addressing the woman in verse two, frustrated that she's caught up in this lame attraction. It reverses the roles Billie Joe and the woman play in 'When I Come Around' where he asks her to be patient. That's a conclusion one might come to without the knowledge of what Billie Joe tweeted: 'That song is about my mother's husband; it's not really about a girl or anyone directly related to me in a relationship. 'In the End''s about my mother.'

'F.O.D.' (Lyrics: Armstrong; Music: Green Day)

After three straight lightning-fast tracks, Armstrong gives Dirnt and Cool a well-deserved two-minute smoke break, to let their steaming, smoking instruments, cool down. Armstrong gets back on acoustic like he did to conclude *Kerplunk*, but it's a trap. This is a spoiler alert – Do not continue reading until you hear this song! After almost two minutes, the band explodes like the atomic bomb blast on the album cover. It's a fantastic and rewarding conclusion to an amazing album.

The title acronym (which stands for 'Fuck off (and) die') is appropriate for the final attack song on *Dookie*. All of the vitriol on the album has added up to a new avenue for Green Day's lyrics to ride. It will come in handy for their follow-up album *Insomniac*, which rides a heavy wave of revenge amidst its physical suffering. Green Day are no longer the innocent sweet children who sang about love. They've made room for hate as well. Similar to the 'Enemius Sleepus' rude awakening, Billie Joe is arguing again with someone he's had fights with in the past, and now just wants to totally give up. Visuals of burning bridges are lumped-in to show these two arguing parties have already tried to quit each other in the past. 'Let's nuke the bridge we torched 2000 times before/This time we'll blow it all to hell,' he sings in the quietude.

In verse two, he gives his opponent a crumb by declaring that some moments were fun, but since the guy is so rotten now, he can't remember the good times with warmth. The music explodes like the bridge Armstrong *nuked*, and Billie Joe lets loose with a curse-filled rant. This narrator feels very comfortable in his anger. It's Green Day's toughest and nastiest song yet.

'All By Myself' (Cool)

This is perhaps the band's most atypical tune. It was written (and sung) by Tré alone – a rare time Green Day was not credited for the music. Tré plays acoustic guitar alone all the way through, with Billie Joe on percussion. It has the goofiest and most adorable lead vocal on any of their songs. It's also their only unlisted track – hidden on the end of 'F.O.D.' and heard only after a few minutes of silence. It was a 1990s trend to hide secret songs on albums.

'All By Myself' uses a seemingly-authentic delivery about someone alone masturbating, while thinking of a girl he likes, adds to the laughter. Tré's voice is hilarious at times, stretching out 'No one was looooking' like he was simultaneously giddy and guilty of committing a small crime. He's leaning over to whisper/sing a secret in our ear. Just setting up the scene's visual, shows how far Tré is willing to play out a joke. 'You and me had such wonderful times... when I was all by myself.'

Non-LP B-sides
'On The Wagon' (Lyrics: Armstrong; Music: Green Day)

This first appeared on the 'Basket Case' single in November 1994. It's much closer to classic rock, being one of the first times they attempted something other than pop punk. The wide-open sound allows more room for Armstrong's tasteful and sparse lead guitar licks. The band adds their favorite dynamic – the stop/start technique – utilizing it masterfully. As a band, they roll alongside the singer at a mid-tempo like they're driving the wagon, and then stop for Billie Joe just when he sings, 'I'm on the wagon again,' and then the band's wagon resumes.

There's some playful sexual humor here, though it's a bit clumsy, but the lyric has some of Armstrong's first wordplay. He takes the expression 'on the wagon,' and twists it so the wagon is really like riding in a relationship. He's been off the wagon for some time, not dating anybody. But in this song, he's back on the wago; his 'love train' is headed for the 'sea of love', to use two classic songs from pop's past, by The O'Jays and The Platters, respectively. The song also appears on the band's B-sides collection *Shenanigans*.

'Tired Of Waiting For You' (Ray Davies)

This 'Basket Case' B-side was Green Day's third cover song. Once again, in their time machine, they head to England for inspiration; back to the 1960s to cover the legendary band The Kinks. Originally released in 1965, it was a number one UK hit that also reached 6 in the US. It may not be as famous as The Who's 'My Generation, 'but it's another significant 1960s rock track. The Kinks song ties in way better with the introverted lyrical personality of Green Day's indie releases. It's a humble song about a man getting impatient waiting for a relationship with the woman he desires. This could be why Adrienne and Billie Joe married so quickly once she'd moved to California after so much waiting: they were tired of waiting. The concept of waiting would prove to be relevant for a few of Green Day's most important songs: like 'Waiting' from *Warning*. This Kinks cover made it to *Shenanigans* as well.

'J.A.R.' (1995 single from the *Angus* soundtrack) (Lyrics: Mike Dirnt; Music: Green Day)

The outstanding motivational speech 'J.A.R.' is one of Green Day's greatest songs. After a brief bass intro, they get down to business with the most underrated hit single of their career. It hit number one on the Modern Rock chart, and was often played in concert at the time, but it's faded from fan memory. The remarkable performance is smartened up by Tré's restraint – sticking to snare, light cymbal hits and hi-hat – Mike's dancing around the charging chunka-chunka guitar lines, and Billie Joe sticks to a bright tone for the instrumental break. The verse and chorus vocal melodies are outstanding. Billie Joe and Mike share the mic for the amazingly-singable chorus. The bridge has another magical melody: one of the most exciting bridges of their career. To conclude the song, Billie Joe sings *a cappella* about future plans to keep your dreams alive. An all-time career highlight, the single continued the band's Green Day's winning streak in the 1990s.

The acronym 'J.A.R.' stands for Jason Andrew Relva: a band friend that passed away in a car accident. Mike Dirnt wrote one of the band's best lyrics as a tribute – detailing their loss by explaining Jason's point of view, how it relates to the listeners' point of view, and how life is fleeting and can disappear at anytime, so it's worth shooting for the stars and making a plan of action for the future. 'J.A.R.' The track appeared on the *Angus* soundtrack in 1995 but was eventually re-released in 2001 on the Green Day compilation *International Superhits*! 'J.A.R.' may be the peak of their 1990s output, proving that Green Day weren't going to just be a one-album wonder to the general public, indicating Billie Joe had a fisherman's jacket worth of melodic hooks fans would be enjoying for years into the future.

Insomniac (1995)

Personnel:
Billie Joe Armstrong: lead vocals, guitar
Mike Dirnt: bass, backing vocals
Tré Cool: drums
Producers: Rob Cavallo, Green Day
Recorded at Hyde Street, San Francisco, California
Label: Reprise
Release date: 10 October 1995
Chart: US: 2, UK: 8
Singles: 'Geek Stink Breath,' 'Brain Stew,' 'Stuck With Me,' 'Walking Contradiction'

Life was now both better and worse for the band. They were the bee's knees to all the new fans and media awoken by *Dookie,* but to the Gilman scene they were originally rooted in, they were now sellouts. They took the backlash hard because they were banned from the club and lost a lot of friends. Billie Joe and Tré got married and had children. But Armstrong has claimed he's more inspired to write about the negative, and besides 'Westbound Sign' – a vignette about his wife Adrienne – Green Day ignore their families in their songs and focus on both the Gilman scene and their internal and external frustrations with themselves and the world.

Insomniac is the first Green Day album to lack a funny novelty track. This protagonist never secured a woman to marry, and never had a child. After all the times Billie Joe pined for a woman in real life and in songs as a teen, now he was 21 and finally had a wife and even a child, he totally dropped the line of thought. This is one reason why *Insomniac* has none of that Lookout-era innocence where fans root for the good guy just trying to find love. *Insomniac* seems to take on somewhat of a villainous role like Billie Joe assumed in 'Having A Blast.' It's as if he's starring in *Nightmares of an Insomniac* – coming to a theater near you. He's cynical, confrontational, bleak and brash, but still knows how to write great melodies and catchy hooks. His vocals are nastier, with nasal snarl, losing that youthful teen voice of earlier records.

The mental anxieties of Green Day's protagonists have now manifested as physical wounds. During their 1994 appearance on KROQ's *Lovelines* show with Dr. Drew, one caller talked about mental anguish affecting the body. The lyrics are filled with physical agonizing, to symbolize mental pain.

If methamphetamine and coffee were the stimulants when recording *Insomniac*, it's clear in the speed and power throughout. The band have never been closer to hardcore punk than they are on these visceral songs. *Insomniac* is around the same length as their first two albums, and almost ten minutes shorter than *Dookie*. It would've been tough for the band and their listeners to go further since – ironically – *Insomniac* is exhausting-enough to cause an insomniac to fall asleep. The unrelentless onslaught matches the lyrics' chaotic distress. But while the band are bigger and badder than ever (thanks to producer Rob Cavallo), they've lost some of their more-intelligent dynamics and intricacies. Tré puts in a mighty turbocharged effort that can dizzy the senses. Billie Joe doesn't add any unique moments or great guitar solos, but his riffage is as fiery and passionate as it's always been. The band have scaled back Mike's role some, with less bass spotlights and harmonies than the last two albums. He's not quite as creative – stepping back to *Kerplunk* heights: which is still great.

'Armatage Shanks' (Lyrics: Armstrong; Music: Green Day)
The pumped-up 'Armatage Shanks' opens with a big hesitating Tré beat, before the band crash through with an angry, fiery, visceral sound that has no time for detail or nuance. It just powers through with its memorable melody and grand chorus hook. The extraordinary dynamics are in place. Tré adds toms and kick drum, and Armstrong does the first of many 'Suh!' vocal ad-libs. Perhaps it's an ad-lib representing 'Suck it!' He used 'Suh!' more frequently live.

Billie Joe might as well have sung, 'I must insist on being a pessimist/ Flush me down the toilet.' The British toilet company Armitage Shanks was the song's inspiration. He'd always been self-deprecating and self-doubting. But on *Insomniac*, all his internal and external frustrations finally come to a head, and Armstrong is suffering greatly. The opening track is an indicator of what's to come. 'Self-loathing freak/An introverted deviant' displays his new dictionary of pain and new level of hate. His humor has greatly darkened with lines like, 'I perfect the science of the idiot.' He told *Rolling Stone* in 1995: 'I'm human still, I'm probably angry at least five days out of a week, just like anybody is. Everybody gets sick of life. It's human nature.' He told *Spin* in 1995:

> It was right before *Dookie* came out, and I was really at odds with myself. I was like, 'Man, do I really want to do this?' A lot of time, I was thinking about suicide, how it's so easy to kill yourself, but it's so hard to stay alive. I was in a breakup with my then-girlfriend – a total raving punk rocker who didn't approve of me being on a major label. She moved down to Ecuador, saying she couldn't live in a world with McDonald's and such. It was fucking me up pretty bad.

'Brat' (Lyrics: Armstrong; Music: Green Day)
After a single *a cappella* vocal line similar to the 'Private Ale' opening, the band storm the gates with more intense rocking. Tré sets up each verse with a thrill-loaded drum fill. It's another catchy number with a great Billie Joe vocal, but the melody sounds rehashed from earlier material working with chords they've used numerous times previously. Another instrumental break reveals a guitar-solo retirement – it's on a permanent vacation.

48

The band jump classes to take down the rich. The protagonist is waiting for his parents to die, so he can gain his inheritance. At first, he admits he thought he could do it on his own, but everything goes wrong, and he gets bored easily. He doesn't want a boring life of going to a job every day. Now that he's given up on himself, he'd rather just be *given* the money.

'Stuck With Me' (Lyrics: Armstrong; Music: Green Day)

Though the album's other three singles overshadowed this one, it's still the closest song to the *Dookie* days, playing like a logical continuation of that album's excellence and entertainment value. It's pretty standard instrumentally, with a no-frills break. The intro is similar to that on 'One Of My Lies.' Dirnt's bass is mostly effective in the refrain, and simpler in the verses. Tré's effort holds his usual greatness matching his power with precision.

The song title is never sung since it's known (though never confirmed) that there was a tape-label mix-up that led to this song being confused with the outtake 'Do Da Da'. Before the error, the tape was named 'Alright,' which makes sense since the word is sung here plenty of times. Eventually, 'Do Da Da' would be issued as a B-side.

The somewhat-successful single is about someone who feels his worth is low when spending time with someone richer who is using him for his or her pleasure. Ironically, Billie Joe jumped from middle class to upper class as Green Day started recording their fourth album due to Dookie's fantastic album sales. He can't take it anymore, and wants out. 'I'm not part of your elite/I'm just alright' begins the track, and by the time he reaches the chorus, he's singing, 'I know I'm not alright.' It doesn't matter how he feels about himself; he'll be 'down-classed by the powers that be' and judged on his economics no matter how he acts. 'Cast out, buried in a hole' and 'Throw me back in the gutter' showcase Armstrong's new lyric device of linking mental-anguish overload with excruciating physical pain.

'Geek Stink Breath' (Lyrics: Armstrong; Music: Green Day)

The successful grunge-like lead single 'Geek Stink Breath' may hold the best chorus hook here, and was a great choice for introducing *Insomniac*. But it again lacks some of the stellar band dynamics featured on *Dookie*. It's straightforward and mighty powerful in this incarnation, just knocking your teeth out with intensity and grit. Dirnt's bass careens off Armstrong's metallic riffage, and Tré keeps things heavy with thumping bass drum and great toms work. Add another Billie Joe 'Suh' ad-lib to the pile.

The excruciating physical pain is on a full museum display in a showcase window with a huge spotlight on it. The video was such an anti-commercial move because they took this lead single and placed it with close-up images of a hideous dental procedure that wound up being too gruesome to stay in MTV's rotation. Banning the video partially prevented mass success for *Insomniac* since the album's other singles didn't chart as high as the *Dookie* ones had.

'Geek Stink Breath' is about the physical toll of methamphetamine – a drug that a Green Day member or two tried at the time. Armstrong uses the experience to warn others that marijuana may be great, but this drug is a no-no, and that his body is crumbling in parallel with his life. 'Geek' is a nickname for 'meth.' Billie Joe uses it like he's a geek or nerd. Unfortunately, many folks didn't listen, since the drug later had a much higher profile, being considered one of the most-murderous narcotics. The gory lyrical visuals include a pimply and pale complexion, rotting teeth, scabs and an inconsistent pulse, matching the video. The dark humor continues when he sings, 'Wish in one hand, shit in the other/And see which one gets filled first.' Like 'Stuck With Me,' it's a stellar single, but not legendary like the *Dookie* singles.

'No Pride' (Lyrics: Armstrong; Music: Green Day)

As fast and potent as 'No Pride' is, somehow it retains its melodic pop. Nothing shakes off the melody and hooks in Green Day songs: even another fiery performance. This would be a single for most pop-punk bands, but here it's just a stand out album track. The instrumental break merely serves as a rest for Billie Joe's voice. As a whole, the songwriting (though not the performance) provides enough excitement. It doesn't matter if there's no solo or quirky effects. Tré uses creative drum fills unconventionally during the choruses instead of waiting until after the vocal lines, and Mike stays with high bass notes, syncopating with the vocal on the refrains.

'No Pride' continues the vicious attacks alluding to the band's so-called 'sellout' status. Billie Joe put extra work into his lyrics as he was learning how to layer and meanings. 'Sects of disconnection and traditions of lost faith/No culture's worth a stream of piss, a bullet in my face,' he sings as he dissects the East Bay punk scene's philosophies. The Gilman crowd had faith, pride, honor and values: all words in this song. But Armstrong is arguing that these normally praiseworthy qualities are weapons of attack to them.

'Well, I am just a mutt, and nowhere is my home,' Billie sings, feeling like he got kicked out of his own house, while 'Dignity's a landmine in the school of lost hope' signifies how impossible it was to have dignity with a punk crowd who will crucify because of their own oversensitivity. 'No Pride' matches Billie Joe's real opinion with the protagonist's voice, singing that the Gilman crowd made him feel like he had no pride to stay in the indie community, linking the song title to the second line where he resigns to 'close my eyes and die.' The song's sick joke sits on an Armitage Shanks – 'You better digest your values, 'cause they turn to shit,' singing about the backwards thinking of Berkeley, California.

'Bab's Uvula Who?' (Lyrics: Armstrong; Music: Green Day)

This quirky hurricane is a riff-based track relying heavily on stop/start rhythm for its verses, which wind the song into a wounded fury before it releases and uncoils its cobra-like attack on the choruses. Mike bolsters the decent chorus hook, but the jet-engine horsepower renders the melody inconsequential. It's the fastest song yet for this already speedy band, and Tré's bass drum adds to its mass.

Though the title stemmed from a *Saturday Night Live* Gilda Radner sketch character, it wasn't any kind of fun song. It's about having a temper due to stress, and the pressure of following up a successful album. Sadly, 'Spontaneous combustion panic attack' is one of the song's true parts, since Billie Joe and especially Mike would experience panic attacks on a regular basis. Armstrong does a great job of using repetition and larger words to better express his tumultuous times. The phrase 'loss of control' became a Green Day song title in the *¡Uno!* era.

'86' (Lyrics: Armstrong; Music: Green Day)

The bitter '86' has the kind of snarling vocal that Billie Joe didn't often attempt in his Lookout days. They also use more guitars, bringing a slight return to the *Kerplunk* feel. It's quiet on the dynamics front, though. It appears *Insomniac* relies more on power than creative intricacy. The band play directly to the root of the problem.

When Green Day were '86'ed – or thrown out of Gilman Street, their home away from home – they momentarily wondered if the band and a major label was worth it but quickly rebounded for this central attack of *Insomniac*. Billie Joe sets the scene at the door of Gilman – acknowledged in the bratty pre-chorus. 'Stand aside and let the next one pass/Don't let the door kick you in the ass,' Billie Joe sings, playing the part of Gilman club owner Tim Yohannan. Though some questioned their 'punk credibility, most Green Day fans were enthusiastic about the group's music. It was just that their original fans were harsh. Yohannan took the brunt of Green Day's aural brutality.

'Panic Song' (Lyrics: Armstrong, Dirnt; Music: Green Day)

This song plays the hero and saves the day for a band that had been amazingly destructive sonically, but creatively quieter than on *Dookie*. They don't just start with a fascinating two-minute buildup made of Pete Townshend windmilling-arm power chords, but the chaotic rhythms that Tré revs up, intensify as they build, and you can just feel the explosion about to happen like a volcano's heat before it blows. When the actual song muscles its way in, it's every bit as monstrous as you'd expect, playing out just like 'F.O.D.,' with dramatic tension and finally a long-anticipated blasting, satisfying release.

The earlier 'Bab's Uvula Who?' caught Billie Joe and Mike in the midst of a major panic attack, and it happens again here. *Apathy to the misery of the world* is the message since caring results in 'Broken glass inside my head/ Bleeding down these thoughts of anguish.' The external-affects-internal theme, intertwines with their mental-affects-physical theme on this dynamic track. The exciting arrangement overshadows the mediocre chorus and even the great verses.

'Stuart And The Ave.' (Lyrics: Armstrong; Music: Green Day)

Like 'Pulling Teeth', 'Stuart And The Ave.' is such a jolly-sounding song that its pessimistic lyric is not a match made in heaven. Armstrong shows no stress, and the band sound handcuffed, sticking too closely to the song, with no change-ups except the occasional drum fill. Luckily, *Insomniac* is so mind-blowing, aurally with its tornado speed, that it didn't matter if the band weren't reaching their full potential.

At times, Billie Joe still liked to set up visual scenes early in songs. Here he's at the corner of Stuart Street and Telegraph Avenue, witnessing a bratty woman break off her relationship with him. Like past love songs, he cuts himself down a notch, but on *Insomniac*, it's only to prove a point in his attack. 'Well, destiny is dead in the hands of bad luck' is another step up in the poetic side of Armstrong's writing. It's another personal song written about Billie Joe's breakup with a woman sometime earlier.

'Brain Stew' (Lyrics: Armstrong; Music: Green Day)

Perhaps the best use of grunge's stop/start dynamic, this song covers various moods, ranging from the boring slurred, slithery, sleepy vocal, to the scratchy guitar breaks that divide the verses from one another. The exciting, grimy grunge finale concludes the most successful and enduring song of *Insomniac*.

With a newborn baby around, Armstrong couldn't get much sleep, and eventually, his insomniac life got to him. But it wasn't just the baby's fault. His experiments with methamphetamine – documented on 'Geek Stink Breath' – had also rattled his brain into a stew. Like the lead single, 'Brain Stew' – the album's most successful single – reads like another list of physical aches and discomforts.

Like many early songs, this track takes place in Billie Joe's bedroom, as we watch him hunched over in delirium with a dry mouth and eyes that feel like they're going to pop out of their sockets. Though his personal life runs parallel to 'Brain Stew' and 'Geek Stink Breath,' both songs take Billie Joe's real meth reactions, and dump a lot of drama into the stew. Brain Stew is the nickname of James Washburn: a longtime band friend. Billie Joe told *Rolling Stone* in 2020:

This song is such a dark horse, about methamphetamine, not being able to sleep, and staying up all night. It was creeping into our punk scene at the time, and I did my experimenting with it. It's just such an evil drug. Things were getting really scary. That sort of fueled that record. Everything was happening. I got married, I had a kid, I was 23 years old, and people were climbing in my trees to look inside my house. It was the scary side of becoming a rock star, or whatever. You can't control the outcome of your life. I wanted to show the uglier side of what Green Day was capable of.

'Jaded' (Lyrics: Armstrong: Music: Green Day)

If 'Brain Stew' was sleepy, 'Jaded' is 'Brain Stew' leaping out of bed, shocked by the ringing sound of a speedy alarm clock. The segue is similar to that between 'Chump' and 'Longview.' 'Jaded' could be a soundtrack to the Coney Island hot dog eating contest. Armstrong can't breathe, and he has to sing so quickly to cram all the words in. Lots of cymbals and one-note bass work, fill this speed-demon track.

Billie Joe's new apocalyptic notions of the world were peaking on *Insomniac*. With music that sounds like a band on speed, he was feeling apocalyptic, like a raging man about to break into lunatic land. 'Countdown from 9 to 5/Hooray, we're gonna die!' shows he could never work a typical everyday job, but then he uses that like he's counting down to the end of the world – just like in 'Having A Blast' – since everything 'turns to shit,' like he sang in 'No Pride.' 'Always move forward', he sings on the chorus. In 1999, he told *Spin* that he 'couldn't go back to the punk scene, whether we were the biggest success in the world or the biggest failure. The only thing I could do, was get on my bike and go forward.'

'Westbound Sign' (Lyrics: Armstrong: Music: Green Day)

Using a somewhat-similar melody to 'The Words I Might Have Ate,' the tuneful 'Westbound Sign' lightens the mood. Because it's for Adrienne, Armstrong doesn't use the nasal snarl as much but just sings with his saliva-filled mouth curling around another great melody. The no-frills look continues as the band barely change the backing, and leave it as is when it hits the bridge. The break only *ups* the guitar count, and loads on more power. Dirnt and Tré add little to the song's décor.

Armstrong wrote this about his wife Adrienne moving to California from Minnesota. They married in summer 1994 as *Dookie* was high on alternative rock fans' priority list. It's a rare 1990s Green Day song that's written in the third person.

Though he doesn't explicitly reveal in the song itself that it's about Adrienne, he gives a hint in the bridge, singing, 'Is tragedy 2000 miles away? – referencing the *Kerplunk* track '2000 Light Years Away': Adrienne's introduction into the Green Day world. 'Will she find her name in the California cement?' is another stellar line that showed Billie Joe was getting better with every album, playing with words, expressions and grammar.

'Tight Wad Hill' (Lyrics: Armstrong: Music: Green Day)

Tight Wad Hill was a seedy section in Crockett, California where drug dealers did business. Billie Joe told *Rolling Stone*: 'This is where all the losers, the cheapskates, would come up and watch the football games without paying for them. It's actually the best view in the whole place. A lot of tweakers come and hang out up here; the crank victims and stuff.' Heavy like the baggage carried by the Tightwad Hill losers, Green Day have never tried to overshadow their melodies more than on Insomniac. There's no time for sonic detail.

This song imagines a 'drugstore hooligan' who makes the spot his outpost. The cheapskate drug dealer ruins the lives of 'white trash mannequins,' as if they're objects and not people.

'Walking Contradiction' (Lyrics: Armstrong: Music: Green Day)

After a tough and menacing buildup, Billie Joe barks out his own profile without a care in the world, as shown in the single's humorous video, where he walks casually through calamity after calamity. He has no guilt in feeling like he can contradict himself or do any crazy things to anyone he feels like, and it shows in his cool, snarky vocal: the best part of the performance. Dirnt stays synced with Billie Joe's chords, and Tré – who hasn't tried anything new for a few songs – is solid.

On *Insomniac*, it's hard to tell if the protagonist is angrier with himself or the world. Either way, he needs to get out and hit a baseball, tackle a football player or hit a golf ball. A sport could've been a good way to handle such pent-up rage.

Non-LP B-sides
'Good Riddance' (Lyrics: Armstrong: Music: Green Day)

This can't be right: 'Good Riddance,' a B-side to 'Brain Stew'? But it is. This is the rare first version. The vocal is a bit more gruff and nasal, but it has the same mood and sentiment as the more famous 1997 version re-recording. Overall, the more-refined remake on *Nimrod* is better. Look for more about the song in that album's chapter.

'Do Da Da' (Lyrics: Armstrong: Music: Green Day)

The standard issue pop-punk 'Do Da Da' and its chorus of 'Stuck with me' is the song that some think was confused in a tape-label mix-up with 'Stuck With Me' from *Insomniac*. It's unclear why this tune is titled 'Do Da Da,' and that may be the reason. It may be one of Billie Joe's most romantic tunes. He asks for forgiveness from a woman (presumably his wife), for all the grief and pain that she has had to endure. 'Oh hang up your soul to my wrists, and I'll vow my trust to you/Moving here, I always said,' he sings to his wife. A 90-second filler that wasn't good enough for *Insomniac,* this is one of the band's weakest 1990s songs. This appears on *Shenanigans*.

'I Want To Be On T.V.' (Sam McBride, Tom Flynn)

While this song needs no dissection (It's just a punk song about wanting to be famous), it not only alleviates the band's usual heavy topics but, for some strange reason, Billie Joe wants to be on a 1980s TV show in the 1990s! The band Fang originally released the song in 1985. It's pretty funny hearing

Armstrong sing about being on the TV show *Solid Gold*, losing his pants in the infamously highly-sexed 1970s New York club Studio 54, and wearing his Calvin Klein jeans while he sniffs his free cocaine. The track's 86 seconds appeared on *Shenanigans* in 2002.

'Don't Wanna Fall in Love' (Lyrics: Armstrong: Music: Green Day)
This speedy track is a humdrum punk shuffle until the odd country guitar solo dips it into Nashville, before heading back to Ramones territory with busy drumming and rambling guitar. A straightforward song about not wanting to fall in love with a particular woman, Armstrong leaves it open as to whether he's just telling her that because he doesn't like her or because he just has no time for love. This was re-released on the B-side compilation, *Shenanigans*.

Nimrod (1997)

Personnel:
Billie Joe Armstrong: lead vocals, guitar; harmonica ('Walking Alone')
Mike Dirnt: bass, backing vocals
Tré Cool: drums, bongos, tambourine, backing vocals
Additional personnel:
Petra Haden: violin ('Hitchin' A Ride', 'Last Ride In')
Conan McCallum: violin ('Good Riddance (Time of Your Life)')
Gabriel McNair, Stephen Bradley, Wayne Bergeron: horns
David Campbell: string arrangements
Producers: Rob Cavallo, Green Day
Recorded at Conway Studios, Los Angeles, California
Label: Reprise
Release date: 14 October 1997
Charts: US: 10, UK: 11
Singles: 'Hitchin' A Ride,' 'Good Riddance (Time of Your Life),' 'Nice Guys Finish Last,' 'Redundant,' 'Scattered'

Green Day's fifth album *Nimrod* is their last of mostly straight pop-punk. The band, Reprise and Rob Cavallo all advertised the album as one of diversity that saw Green Day move in new directions. But in reality, of the 18 songs totaling almost 50 minutes, maybe only three held significant change – the crossover-ballad chart hit 'Good Riddance (Time Of Your Life)'; the ska track 'King For A Day,' which they dress up with brass, and the surf instrumental 'Last Ride In' that sits in the middle of the album, cutting the rest into pop-punk halves. The remaining songs are territory they've covered before, but with slight twists, like the bouncy 'Hitchin' A Ride' with its brief horn intro, the speed-metal 'Take Back,' and the harmonica-laden 'Walking Alone.' They do up the adventure quotient for their pop-punk songs, once again adding those flourishes that make them one of punk's all-time creative forces. Billie Joe told the *Toronto Star* in 1997: 'We wanted to change a little bit; not dramatically. The point of this album is to have a wider range, and I think it ranges from the most aggressive stuff we've ever done to the prettiest stuff we've ever done.'

In the 2013 documentary *Cuatro*, he off-handedly mentioned he'd written the *Nimrod* lyrics in the studio, but it was something he never wanted to do again. The lyrics are angry and bitter, like *Insomniac*, but they are less general and more-focused aggravation.

Billie Joe told *Spin* in 1997: 'All the love songs on *Nimrod* are about Adrienne. But even the love songs are not necessarily happy songs, so they might piss her off.' Some lyrics take on a new subject: alcohol dependency. Armstrong told *Rolling Stone* in 2014:

> Some people can go out, have a couple of drinks, and they can take it or leave it. I couldn't predict where I was going to end up at the end of the

night. I've been trying to get sober since 1997: right around *Nimrod*. But I didn't want to be in any programs. Sometimes, being a drunk, you think you can take on the whole world by yourself. This (a 2012 iHeart Radio incident) was the last straw.

With the prolific approach came lower-quality songwriting, which hinders the album some. They do reach peaks of inspiration and quality, as the two classic singles – the successful 'Hitchin' A Ride' and 'Good Riddance (Time of Your Life)' – indicate. But the remainder – even the promo singles – never feel like a captivating experience. They're always worthwhile, they're always professional, but the weaker *Nimrod* tracks don't possess the pizzazz. In hindsight, Armstrong somewhat agreed, telling *Guitar World* in 2000: 'Our last album was written by just pounding-out songs. We took any idea and finished the tune no matter what.'

'Nice Guys Finish Last' (Lyrics: Armstrong; Music: Green Day)
Though *Nimrod* was cited as a new creative endeavor, Green Day sound familiar on the great opener: the single, 'Nice Guys Finish Last'. Their sound is still fresh when their stellar songwriting. They start whipping up a fresh batch with this somewhat-successful single: a fun, energetic track. Dirnt alternates between high and low notes while Tré beats up the drum kit in star fashion.

Armstrong informed *Spin* in 1997: 'When you've got managers and lawyers crawling up your ass, everybody thinks they know what's best for you. It's like nice guys finish last.' Titled after that aphorism, the lyric insists on being pessimism, philosophising that being kind results in susceptibility. Verse one targets the 'nice guy' who shouldn't pat himself on the back, because his spine will break. It's more of Billie Joe's dry and dark humor twisting another aphorism by making it literally a physical pat. Bad guys think nice guys have a weak spine – or in other words, are short on confidence. Verse two targets the bad guy, who doesn't have a care in the world. The pre-chorus reveals that the singer is on the bad side since he's so happy he can cry. 'Pressure cooker, bake my brain, and tell me I'm insane' has Armstrong bring back his old mental instability days. Ultimately, the band provides a hot performance on this pressure-cooker opener.

'Hitchin' A Ride' (Lyrics: Armstrong; Music: Green Day)
The most well-known *Nimrod* number is a thumping powerhouse; an excellent composition with stellar dynamics. Violinist Petra Haden starts the track, leading into Tré's powering rhythm that bounds and pounds like a bear. Mike and Billie Joe hitch a ride on Tré's drums, and all three being in sync, the throbbing rhythm swells to titanic proportions. 'My tongue is swelling up I say, shit!' Armstrong blows his top vocally in the quiet, leading to another sonic dream, peak-production pleasure. The chorus is Green Day at their most lethal, blazing through one of their best refrains. They annihilate

everything around with their most exciting instrumental moment this side of 'Panic Song' and 'F.O.D.'. It's a world-size sonic explosion that adds a knockout punch to an amazing lead single that remains a memorable Green Day classic, years later.

Billie Joe continues to stride towards a career as a poet, as he's finding some magic in his pen. Like 'Welcome To Paradise,' 'Hitchin' A Ride' is another major turning point in his lyrics. He plays with language like he's fully in control while also improving his vocabulary. Maybe he could've been a great high school student. This is one of Armstrong's most clever lyrics. The singer needs help getting *back on the wagon*, or returning to a more normal, sober life. Previously, Green Day sung about love in 'Private Ale,' and the love song 'On The Wagon' used the same common saying to refer to getting back into relationships.

In verse one, his use of homonyms could have confused listeners if he wasn't as adept at using them as he had become. 'Need a lift to happy hour?' Armstrong, as the driver asks; the protagonist responds, 'Do you brake for distilled spirits?/I need a break as well/The well that inebriates the guilt.' Armstrong substitutes 'alleviate' for 'inebriate,' creating his own expression from an existing one. It's a trick he'd use successfully through a lot of the *Warning* and *American Idiot* albums.

Armstrong's playful nature with words and common phrases continues in verse two with lines like, 'Cold turkey's growing stale/Tonight I'm eating crow' and 'There's a drought at the fountain of youth/Now I'm dehydrated.' All of it points to our protagonist giving in to alcohol. Instead of getting back on the wagon to ride life sober, he's hitchin' the wagon that's on its way to a bar.

'The Grouch' (Lyrics: Armstrong: Music: Green Day)

Keeping it simple like on their last album, 'The Grouch' is played straightforwardly, letting Billie Joe's whiny grumbling be the star of this brisk, brash track. They work over a fast rhythm, with Mike laying out sparse bass notes, and Billie Joe brightening the tone of the guitar break.

The lyric growth continues as Billie Joe takes on the persona of a old curmudgeon that wasted his life and blames the world. He has no 'glory days' to remember so he 'drinks a six-pack of apathy,' which harkens back to the 'Hitchin' A Ride' alcohol theme by subbing the word 'beer' for the word 'apathy.' He'd rather just drink and forget about his miserable life.

'Redundant' (Lyrics: Armstrong; Music: Green Day)

Taking a break from all the pop-punk of the last few albums, the band here slow down, calm down, lower the volume and aggression, and find themselves in the classic-rock world. There's even a Leslie-speaker guitar effect. The melody and hooks lead the way, but they stall on the road. Armstrong provides a purposely-lackadaisical vocal, except when he emotes effectively on the refrain. He told *Spin* in 1997: 'There are things that I can't talk about, that I can only communicate about through a song. Sometimes I can't express the way I feel at home, so I'll demo something and say, 'Hey, Adrienne, listen to this'.' Armstrong finds different ways of saying that being a husband and father has become more of a challenge. In the chorus, he tries to calm his spouse with 'I love you,' but it's lost the original weight it had, feeling like an empty apology.

'Scattered' (Lyrics: Armstrong; Music: Green Day)

They pick up speed as they ride down memory lane for the moderately successful single and reflective *Nimrod* highlight. 'Scattered' contains one of the album's strongest melodies, despite it sounding as if lifted from 'Without You' – written in 1970 by Pete Ham and Tom Evans of Badfinger, and covered famously by Harry Nilsson in 1971 and Mariah Carey in 1993. Mike and Billie Joe properly release themselves of any anger vocally, and deliver an honorable effort. Then again, Mike's not getting as much room to provide amazing bass breaks like he did on *Dookie*.

The majority of Green Day's 1990s songs have been written in the present tense. Some have tried to predict the future. Like 'I Was There' and '409 In Your Coffeemaker,' 'Scattered' heavily focuses on the theme of time being intertwined. 'I've got some scattered pictures lying on my bedroom floor,' has listeners revisiting his bedroom yet again as he tries to solve life's mysteries. He says, 'Open the past and present, and the future too,' as if he's addressing Adrienne, reminding her that they've been through a lot together, so these troubled times are a hurdle they can successfully leap.

Armstrong plays further with literal/figurative and mental/physical themes: 'Well, loose ends tied in knots, leaving a lump in my throat.' The loose ends tied in knots, references when someone takes sheets and knots them together into a rope to climb out of a bedroom window down to the ground, like a kid escaping to see their friends or partner. The knots are literal and metaphorical, but the lump in his throat is figurative as if Adrienne is trying to escape their relationship, and he's feeling choked up. It also connects to his loss for words on 'Redundant.' 'We'll drag it on and on 'til my skin's ripped into shreds' reminds us of the mental-anguish-equals-physical-anguish *Insomniac* method. The photos remind him that's he made mistakes, and if he can change in the future, it can be as great as the past.

'All The Time' (Lyrics: Armstrong; Music: Green Day)

The riff-based 'All The Time' has a raucous rhythm lifting the song some, but it covers the relatively weak vocal melody. Billie Joe talk/sings a lot of it. Dirnt and Cool do a better job of sneaking in some slight rhythmic changes as the metallic elements speed forward. Tré remains tom-happy, and Dirnt sits at home with plenty of high bass notes.

The alcoholic theme resumes in a song about trying to quit drinking, but 'down the hatch' the drinks go. He speaks of New Year's resolutions, promises that don't come true, and how he's wasting his time. He's already wasted time on 'Pulling Teeth,' and here he's enjoying time.

'Worry Rock' (Lyrics: Armstrong; Music: Green Day)

The guitar works well on this worry-wart rocker: one of Green Day's lower-profile songs. Armstrong syncs his vocal with the rhythm, resulting in a lack of emotion in the unusually deep and nasal vocal, though it benefits the bright-toned guitar solo by contrast. Dirnt's loping bass line is the first to heavily benefit a song on *Nimrod*.

It's the first time Billie Joe is consistently writing from inside a relationship, when in the past, he' craved one from the outside. He makes the 'worry rock' a physical entity on the line 'the worry rock has turned to dust and fallen on our pride' and completes the line figuratively. As he said, *Nimrod* love songs are about Adrienne, so this is another song like 'Redundant': detailing his marital stress. 'Fat lips and open wounds' continues his reliance on the physical as a metaphor for emotional turmoil. Again he's open to working it out but finds it frustrating.

'Platypus (I Hate You)' (Lyrics: Armstrong; Music: Green Day)

The venomous 'Platypus' has a lot of sting and bite ground up in its turbo engines. The performance may eat you alive, it's so dastardly evil in its menacing aggression. It piledrives everything in its path, leaving a fiery road, singed by reckless abandon. It's a blistering blur of a sonic tornado. That the band maintains remarkable precision amidst the aural chaos is remarkable. The stellar menacing guitar on the bridge leads into an adventurous – albeit brief – eastern motif.

Supposedly about Tim Yohannan of the Gilman days, the song is a venomous attack with extra power like the tracks on *Insomniac*. Because the band truly felt the lyrics, it may sit as the ugliest angry song in their catalog. Yohannan was their toughest critic and unceremoniously kicked them out of their favorite live-show hot spot. Considering that the alternative rock bands NOFX and The Lead also trashed him in songs, Yohannan may not have been the nicest guy. 'What goes around is coming back and haunting you' is one of the most vicious and apathetic lines in Armstrong's career. Green Day had found out Tim had cancer and was dying before the song was created. He passed away in early 1998: months after *Nimrod*. The lyric was so vicious Green Day's lawyers advised them not to print them in the booklet. The platypus is a poisonous mammal that – ironically – is currently endangered.

'Uptight' (Lyrics: Armstrong; Music: Green Day)

Metallic chugging guitars are poured into the foundation of 'Uptight' – a track that winds up into an uptight state with all the layered riffage, only to break open and out of the sonic bonds with a highly melodic chorus. It's the same tension-and-release dynamic found on 'F.O.D.' and 'Panic Song.' It seems like there's one per album. The chorus has the band in full throttle peeling rubber, and Billie Joe repeats it one or twice too often, and it becomes a bit monotonous. Perhaps this was a suitable time for a fade.

'Uptight' gets us back on track with one of the album's two main themes: Billie Joe's marital issues. On 'Worry Rock,' he mentioned that if he can avoid dead-end streets, their marriage will have the open road to happiness. But 'Uptight' has him singing the oxymorons, 'I got another new start on a dead-end road' and 'Peaked-out on reaching new lows.' It's another song that opens in his bedroom, as he 'woke up 'on the wrong side of the floor,' to acknowledge he passed out drinking the night before.

'Last Ride In' (Green Day)
This is the band's first instrumental, and their first time doing surf rock. It has Dick Dale-style surf guitar, vibraphone and sweet, optimistic horns similar to a 1960s Dionne Warwick track. It's a mood they haven't accomplished since: serenity laced with fear. This is the kind of diversity they advertised before the album's release. After all the problems and hard-driving material, they decided to let their new instinct ride the waves. Tré displays restraint, keeping a smooth mid-tempo groove, and Mike provides an ocean-wave vibe. It's a well-thought-out piece, that moves forward uniquely, incorporating the instruments, so they decorate the main motif in a captivating way. It works for the album like a relaxing halftime break.

'Jinx' (Lyrics: Armstrong; Music: Green Day)
The weak 'Jinx' goes right back to the typical pop-punk. It's professional but indistinctive.

The album's second half reveals that the calm ocean-surfing of 'Last Ride In' hasn't helped the band's situation much. 'I fucked up again and it's all my fault,' Armstrong begins, taking the blame like in so many early Green Day songs. 'Read me my rights and tell me I'm wrong' continues the oxymoron streak. 'You finally met your nemesis, disguised as your long lost love' is another line that may be referencing Adrienne. Billie Joe feels like he's cursed, and it's messing up his life as well as hers.

'Haushinka' (Lyrics: Armstrong; Music: Green Day)
'Jinx' and 'Haushinka' are played continuously, but there's no explanation why. Tré finds a more sparse rhythm that thrusts forward, steps back and thrusts forward again. Billie Joe's distinctive metallic guitar opens the track. The verse and chorus are reliable, but the bridge is rich in melodic content. When they come out of the brief break, the guitar takes on the 'Walking Contradiction' melody, if only for a bit.

Our narrator feeds us the profile of a girl named Haushinka, who he met the day before his birthday (Billie Joe's birthday is 17 February). Supposedly, he met her during Green Day's tour of Japan. It's a basic *what-if* love song. It was originally demoed for *Dookie* in 1993.

'Walking Alone' (Lyrics: Armstrong; Music: Green Day)

The sound of a harmonica greets us on this overburdened and ultimately forgettable pop/rock track. The mediocre composition could have benefited from a great Mike bass line or a vocal harmony. He and Tré, perhaps, are too heavyhanded for this relaxed track, sticking too close to Green Day's typical sound.

Buried on the latter half of this 18-track album, this low-profile track has been totally overshadowed since 2004's more-famous lonely walk 'Boulevard Of Broken Dreams.' The humble narrator here tells us he's made many mistakes he regrets and needs time to reflect and humble himself by taking a stroll. 'Walk on eggshells on my own stomping ground,' again refers to the Gilman scene. He's 'too drunk' to notice that the people he knew from the scene, are no longer there. In the chorus, he sings, 'Sometimes I still feel like I'm walking alone.' The line probably refers to marital trouble. He figures the answer may be to stay humble, keep negativity away, apologize and ask for forgiveness.

'Reject' (Lyrics: Armstrong; Music: Green Day)

We continue through a redundant and monotonous area of *Nimrod* that drops the album's overall quality to below that of their previous work. 'Reject' is humdrum pop-punk. Even the bass-rumble stop/start moment late in the song doesn't help or deviate far from the rhythm. It has the feel of an *Insomniac* leftover. They are starting to paint themselves into a corner with pop-punk.

Some fans think 'Reject' was a response to a fan's angry mother who thought the band were offensive, but it's unclear. The song is just a general attack that could be about anyone. The protagonist does infer the subject of the attack is wealthy and acknowledges some fault of his own, telling the antagonist he'll see them in hell.

The phrase 'reject all-American' was a reference to the title of Riot Grrrl band Bikini Kill's fourth album. Billie Joe told *Billboard* in 1997: 'I really liked the way Bikini Kill's last record came out. They have some really rough punk songs and these delicate, pretty songs.' The phrase may also be the first tiny seed of the eventual idea for *American Idiot*.

'Take Back' (Lyrics: Armstrong; Music: Green Day)

This is total Green Day annihilation hard-core punk or even speed metal, with Billie Joe grown into a ferocious monster growling. He's snarling through his snorting and geek-stink-breath teeth. The words can't even be made out, and it's over in 69 seconds. Still, it's one of the band's biggest, baddest bullies, even if it's the really short and stocky type. Tré is outstanding, and Mike is right there all the way on one of their fastest songs.

'Lights out, I can't take anymore,' Billie Joe barks as if he's still on a rampage igniting the dynamite to rid himself of 924 Gilman's Tim Yohannan. 'Take Back' seems like a minute-long reprise of the blood-spitting 'Platypus.'

'King For A Day' (Lyrics: Armstrong; Music: Green Day)

If 'Take Back' was a bully, 'King For A Day' could be its likely victim. It's a song about embracing sexual curiosity. It's Green Day's only ska excursion, and it happened to arrive right after the ska band No Doubt was getting popular. The brass blows delightfully over a fresh and more-loose pop-punk. The chanted group vocal is a fun moment, and the speed helps the silliness since it serves as one big wild party where anything goes. Despite the weak melody, the fun and enjoyable energy is so invigorating after so much negativity and turbulence; it's welcome colorful relief.

The band's first novelty song since the hidden *Dookie* track 'All By Myself' is about a four-year-old who's curious about trying on his mother's clothing. The kid's father puts him in therapy because he thinks something is wrong with his son. A cute visual of 'G.I. Joe in pantyhose' caps off the only *Nimrod* song that seems uplifting and optimistic.

'Good Riddance (Time Of Your Life)' (Lyrics: Armstrong; Music: Green Day)

This song outshines everything on the album, and almost totally disregards its sound, having just acoustic guitar, a fragile, heartfelt vocal and lovely strings. This is a re-recording of the 'Brain Stew' B-side and is clearly the most famous recording of the two.

Known as a thoughtful song reflecting on the best times in life, in reality, it's Billie Joe's kiss-off letter to Amanda – his ex-girlfriend and inspiration for multiple songs, including 'Chump,' 'She' and 'Sassafras Roots.' As one of the band's best and most-significant songs for the growth of their music, in the long run, it's better to let Billie Joe do the explaining in his 2020 *Rolling Stone* interview:

I wrote this back when I was writing for *Dookie*. It was for a girlfriend who was moving to Ecuador. 'Tattoos of memories and dead skin on trial.' I had tattooed her name on me, and then I had to get it covered up, that's all that was. It's about trying to be cool, accepting that, in life, people go in different directions. People come into your life and it's wonderful, but they seem to go out of your life as quickly as they came in. That's what the song's about ... We put this little string quartet on it, which was going way outside what Green Day was known for. And it was amazing. It opened up a brand new world: 'Oh, fuck, we can do so much more.' It took on a life of its own. I was definitely not thinking about weddings and graduations when I wrote it. A girl just sent me a message on my Instagram – she had a brother that just passed away, and that became the song her family would listen to that they related to their experience. It's really beautiful when you think about it.

Sometimes, time and location affect your destiny, is a way to sum up the opening couplet. There's a philosophy that when we die is when we learn why we're living as humans on Earth, and that we're not meant to know beforehand. The second couplet deals with this, and Armstrong's answer is that we should make the most of our lives, and not prioritize the question. He calls life a 'test,' as if to say, 'If we pass, we'll go to heaven, but if we fail, we'll go to hell.' Life may seem tumultuous, but at the end of our lives, we'll realize why everything worked out the way it did. He hopes we're all enjoying life. But to Amanda, he's just being sarcastic. 'So take the photographs and still frames in your mind/Hang it on a shelf in good health and good time' is the most gracious way to break off a relationship – by reminding a partner that, though it's over, they had great times that they won't forget. He wishes her good health and a good time for her life. 'For what it's worth, it was worth all the while' is a beautiful sentiment, as Billie Joe once more takes a common saying and adds his own signature stamp.

This song has been covered many times and used in movies and television: including the final *Seinfeld* episode.

'Prosthetic Head' (Lyrics: Armstrong; Music: Green Day)
Other than the bass being louder in the mix, there's not much to distinguish this verbal attack from the other *Nimrod* pop-punk mannequins lined up. It's a fine track, with Tré performing wonderfully, but it lacks greatness.

'Another white-trash mannequin,' Billie Joe sang on 'Tight Wad Hill', and here 'Prosthetic Head' indicates a mannequin that can't think for itself – a metaphor for a person who follows what everyone else is doing, and feels soulless. Lack of individualism will be touched on greatly on the next two albums. 'Plastic eyes looking through a numb skull' harnesses that 1960s counterculture opinion of 'plastic people,' or people that are phonies. 'Red-blooded a-mannequin' plays off the phrase 'red-blooded American.' This final assault pushes *Nimrod* towards perhaps being as much of a violently angry record as *Insomniac*.

Related tracks
'Desensitized' (Lyrics: Armstrong; Music: Green Day)
A bell ringing is the first sound we hear on the meaty 'Desensitized'. Then we hear a guy getting beaten up, with lots of things being banged and thrown around the studio: a silly moment of mock aggression. The stop/start riff kicks into gear, but the background craziness doesn't stop. It's one of the band's most creative openings, and once they force their way in and save the poor, beaten guy, the sound cuts so sharply that we may have to watch out for a beheading. Armstrong sings in the pockets of the stop/start rhythm,

Above: Tré Cool, Billie Joe Armstrong, Mike Dirnt in the 1994 'Welcome to Paradise' video. (*Robert Caruso/Reprise*)

Below: Touring guitarists Jason White, Jeff Matika, plus Billie Joe, Tré, touring multi-instrumentalist Jason Freese and Mike playing live in Germany in 2017. (*Alvaronstrong*)

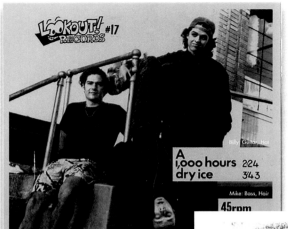

Left: The beginning of Green Day's recording career and their only 1980s release, the *1000 Hours* E.P. *(Lookout)*

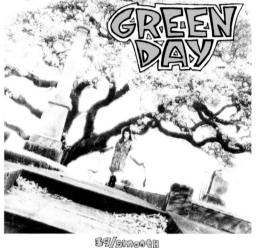

Right: The cover of Green Day's first album, *39/Smooth*, released in 1990. *(Lookout)*

Left: The *Slappy* E.P. with Jason Relva's dog Slappy, issued in 1990. *(Lookout)*

Right: *Sweet Children*, Green Day's third E.P., the title referencing their initial band name. *(Skene!)*

Left: The independent label release that eventually sold 4 million copies, *Kerplunk*. *(Lookout)*

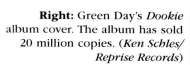

Right: Green Day's *Dookie* album cover. The album has sold 20 million copies. (*Ken Schles/ Reprise Records*)

Left: Mike Dirnt and Billie Joe Armstrong promoting their new album *39/Smooth* at Pinole Valley High School in Pinole, California, 1990. (*Mickey Estes*)

Right: Billie Joe Armstrong in Green Day's first music video 'Longview' from 1994. (*Mark Kohr/Reprise*)

Left: Billie Joe Armstrong in the 1994 'Basket Case' video. (*Mark Kohr/Reprise*)

Above: Billie Joe, Tré and Mike are blissfully unaware of the police car flipping in the 'Walking Contradiction' video. (*Roman Coppola/ Reprise*)

Above: Armstrong and Dirnt on stage live at the V98 Festival in Hylands Park, Chelmsford, England, 1998. (*LatinAutor – Warner Chappel*)

Right: Armstrong, Cool, and Dirnt on their Green Day float in the 2000 'Minority' video. (*Evan Bernard/Reprise*)

Left: Mike Dirnt, Billie Joe Armstrong, and Tré Cool on the 1994 'Basket Case' CD single cover. (*Richie Bucher/Ken Schles/Reprise*)

Right: Green Day's 1995 album *Insomniac* features a collage by Winston Smith called, 'God Told Me To Skin You Alive.' (*Winston Smith/Reprise Records*)

Left: Green Day's *Nimrod* album cover from 1997. *(Reprise)*

Right: *Warning*, the band's transitional album from 2000. *(Reprise)*

Left: Green Day's iconic *American Idiot* album cover from 2004. (*Chris Bilheimer/ Reprise Records*)

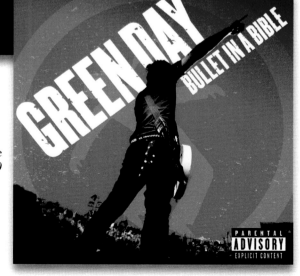

Right: *Bullet in a Bible*, the band's first live album. *(Reprise)*

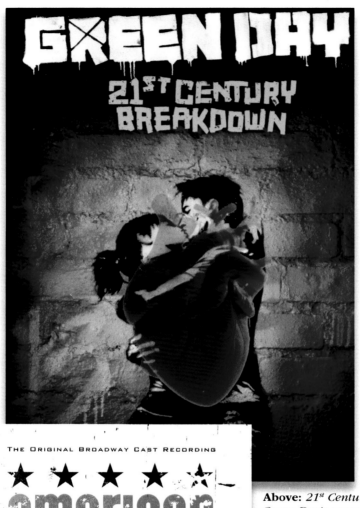

Above: *21st Century Breakdown*, Green Day's second 'rock opera'. *(Reprise)*

Left: Green Day's *American Idiot* album as recreated by the Broadway cast of the hit musical. *(Reprise)*

Right: Tré, Billie Joe, touring member Jason Freese and Mike are live and silly at the Bizarre Festival in Cologne, Germany in 2001. (*LatinAutor – Warner Chappel*)

Left: The 'American Idiot' music video with Green Day in front of the U.S. flag. (*Samuel Bayer/ Reprise*)

Below: Green Day promoting *American Idiot* at the Reading Festival 2004 in England. (*ITV/Rod Wardell*)

Above: Jason White, Billie Joe Armstrong, Tré Cool, Mike Dirnt at the Bell Center in Montreal, Canada 2009. (*Anirudh Kohl*)

Left: Tré screaming live in Ottawa 2009. (*Ceedub*)

Left: Mike Dirnt on stage in Montreal during 2009 promoting *21st Century Breakdown*. (*Anirudh Koul*)

Right: Jason Freese and Billie Joe Armstrong playing 'King For a Day' in 2009. (*Punxie89*)

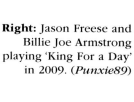

Left: Tré Cool live in 2009 promoting *21st Century Breakdown*. (*Ceedub*)

Right: Jason White and Billie Joe feeling the heat in Scotiabank Place in Ottawa, 2009. (*Ceedub*)

Left: Green Day with Jason White and Jason Freese in their hometown Oakland, California at the Fox Theater in 2009. (*Cafarm*)

Right: Armstrong, Cool, and Dirnt on the *21ˢᵗ Century Breakdown* World Tour in 2010 at Comerica Park in Detroit, Michigan. (*E Carter Sterling*)

Left: Touring multi-instrumentalist Jason Freese blowing saxophone and Billie Joe going Egyptian for 'King For a Day' in 2010 at the Comcast Theater in Hartford, Connecticut in 2010. (*Kimm613*)

Right: Billie Joe Armstrong on the cover of *Uno* from 2013. *(Reprise)*

Left: Mike Dirnt on the *Dos*, the second album of the 'Green Day Trilogy'. *(Reprise)*the band live in the studio in March 1974. *(Bacillus)*

Right: Tré Cool on the cover of *Tré*, the final album of the 'Green Day Trilogy'. *(Reprise)*

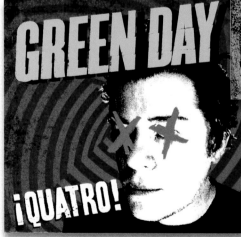

Left: Jason White on the cover of the DVD *Cuatro*, the making of the three 2013 Green Day albums. *(Reprise)*

Left: Billie Joe leaping with a fan on stage live in 2013 at the Rock Im Ring Festival. (*Sven Sebastian Sajak*)

Right: Mike live on stage in 2013 at the Rock Im Ring Festival. (*Sven Sebastian Sajak*)

Left: In the studio with Jason White, Mike, Billie Joe, Ted Jensen, and longtime Green Day producer Rob Cavallo from 2014. (*Ted Jensen*)

Right: Billie Joe and a fan scream for more Green Day at Rock am Ring, Nürburgring, Nürburg, Rheinland-Pflaz, Germany in June, 2022. (*Sven Mandel*)

Left: Mike at Rock am Ring, Nürburgring, Nürburg, Rheinland-Pflaz, Germany in June, 2022. (*Sven Mandel*)

Right: Tré at Rock am Ring, Nürburgring, Nürburg, Rheinland-Pflaz, Germany in June, 2022. (*Sven Mandel*)

Left: Green Day's stellar comeback album, *Revolution Radio* from 2016. (*Nick Spanos/ Reprise Records*)

Right: The humorous greatest hits cover taken from a comment by late-night T.V. host Stephen Colbert. (*Reprise*)

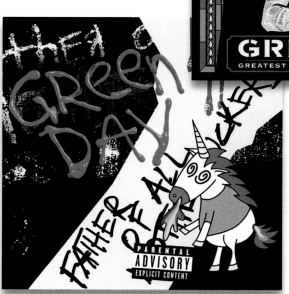

Left: Green Day issued *Father of All Motherf**kers* in the 2020s, fifth decade to see a release by the band. (*Reprise*)

which provides explosive power between verses and choruses. While the verses are mostly spoken, the chorus is surprisingly catchy for a random B-side, upping this to perhaps one of their top-five B-sides. (It was also a bonus track on the Japanese issue of *Nimrod*.) This enormous sound can barely be stuffed into an arena.

Billie Joe takes on the persona of a man who feels like he's going to hell, so to hell with everybody else: just like in 'Having A Blast.' It's a social commentary on how many of us have been desensitized to violence, illness and death due to media and apathetic people around us. 'Another fatal wreck on the information highway' is the song's best line, predicting how confrontational and narcissistic the internet is. He talks of desiring to see acts of violence like a black comedy, but without the laughs.

'Suffocate' (Lyrics: Armstrong; Music: Green Day)
The exciting 'Suffocate' could've easily found a home on *Nimrod*, but it was saved as a B-side: one of their best. It ended up opening the B-side compilation *Shenanigans*. The hooks and vocal melody are passionate and inspired, barely giving the listener a minute to breathe, with Tré pounding out another rapid-fire rhythm. Somehow, Billie Joe can hold it together, and he pumps out another great vocal, loaded with his usual confrontational attitude. Mike drives the verses, and sings a high harmony prominently on various sections.

Combining the gross visuals of *Insomniac* with the alcoholism theme of *Nimrod*, Billie Joe is back at it again, opening with '3 a.m. I'm drunk again/My head is standing underneath my feet/So make it stop, I'm getting off/Sedatives and dizzy spells.' He continues down a laundry list of physical ailments representing mental anguish. 'Give me shelter/Give me give me something' is a nod to The Rolling Stones, wondering when the world can stop rotating so he can jump off before he suffocates. Yes, it's a lot of torment, Billie Joe-style.

'You Lied' (Lyrics: Armstrong; Music: Green Day)
On this *Nimrod* B-side, two guitar parts split, going off in their own directions. It's one of the first times multiple guitar tracks are noticeable, and adds to the band's chemistry. One sticks to a slamming rhythm, and the other rides over the top, then plays a unique solo. It's a great rocker, but it lacks some melody. Dirnt puts in a thoughtful bass effort on the chorus.

Bands that love playing punk tend to create *liar*-attack songs, usually explaining how their target lacks authenticity or credibility. Running down the punk-rock liar song list, we have the Sex Pistols' 'Liar' and The Damned's 'Liar'; D.O.A. had 'Liar For Hire,' The Clash had 'Deny' with a 'You're a liar' chorus, and Henry Rollins Band had the 1990s hit 'Liar'.

'Espionage' (Green Day)
'Espionage' sounds like its title – a spy tune. It fits right into the band's more-colorful *Nimrod* sound, and it hits the right notes. It's intense, menacing, a

little playful, tough and highly effective. It's similar to James Bond music, and after its issue as the 'Hitchin' A Ride' B-side, it was included in *Austin Powers: The Spy Who Shagged Me*. The horns add to the song's sneaky, deceitful character. You can picture the band hiding in the shadows in trench coats as they tiptoe their way to more clues.

'Sick Of Me' (Lyrics: Armstrong; Music: Green Day)
This B-side deserves its role since it's not quite original. Green Day reuse their own melodies, like the 'Walking Contradiction' moment in the instrumental break, and a recycling of the 'Do Da Da' melody serving as the chorus. One may get sick of the leftovers on this forgettable tune that lacks anything but speed.

The song retreads ground covered on a few *Nimrod* songs that detail Armstrong's family issues. The protagonist wants his girlfriend (or Billie Joe wants his wife) to admit she's sick of him, and by the end of the song, he says he's sick of her too. The topics are all rehashed. He has bad habits, lying, losing faith in a relationship, having health loss, and attempts at rekindling. Armstrong purposely sings 'sick of me' after every line, to drive home the point and annoy the listener, until we are also sick of him. The best part is when the band stops playing to fart before jumping right back into the rhythm!

'Rotting' (Lyrics: Armstrong; Music: Green Day)
'I'm rotting inside/My flesh turns into dust,' Billie Joe sings, straightforwardly reliving one of his *Insomniac* nightmares on this B-side, as he states how upset he is by melodramatically proclaiming he's dying. With a lazy vocal straight out of 'Rest,' he sounds wasted, but he's trying a deeper, tired voice that doesn't work. The song seems forced, and even the band don't sound as tight as normal. The lighter touch they're attempting is still too heavy, and the recycling of Armstrong's woes was a sign that the band had found itself out of ideas for the time being. 'Rotting' makes it easy to understand why Green Day took off a couple of years after *Nimrod*.

'The Ballad Of Wilhelm Fink' (Green Day)
Green Day closed an incredible decade of excellent songs with this, the shortest track of their career. The Fat Wreck Chords compilation *Short Songs For Short People* took a page out of the 1980s band The Minutemen's playbook of 60-second-long songs by having artists record 30-second songs. Billie Joe wants to have a little overnight adventure with a woman but is so weary of his bad luck that he figures he'll get arrested before he gets to have sex with her. It's just Billie Joe with an acoustic guitar.

Warning (2000)

Personnel:
Billie Joe Armstrong: lead vocals, guitar, harmonica, mandolin
Mike Dirnt: bass, backing vocals; Farfisa organ ('Misery')
Tré Cool: drums, percussion, accordion
Additional personnel:
Benmont Tench: vocals ('Church On Sunday')
Gary Meek: saxophone ('Jackass')
Mistress Simone: dominatrix
Producer: Green Day
Recorded at Studio 880, Oakland, California
Label: Reprise
Release date: 3 October 2000
Charts: US: 4, UK: 4
Singles: 'Warning,' 'Minority,' 'Waiting,' 'Macy's Day Parade'

Warning is a warming of Green Day's sound and attitude. A lot has changed since *Nimrod,* and from here on out, the band and Billie Joe would write about anything, using different contexts in varying styles. 'Good Riddance (Time of Your Life)' gave them the faith to experiment – not because they felt more confident; they were already confident, but confidence in their fan's willingness to accept softer material. Armstrong has made a ton of headway lyrically on every album. He had opened up the world to find more subjects to sing about. He told the website Blue Railroad: 'That kind of came all together at the same time. I think lyrics on this record were really important to me – and to have a well-rounded record as far as what kind of topics I wanted to write about and sing about. That was one of those songs that seemed to just write itself. It just came really naturally.'

In 2020, he told the *NME*: 'I think we have transitional records. When I look back now, on both *Nimrod* and *Warning*, we were pushing ourselves in a different direction. Without those records, there wouldn't have been an *American Idiot* or *21st Century Breakdown*. It's about trying to push things in a new direction all the time.'

Dirnt told *Rolling Stone* in 2017: 'When it came out, people were like, 'What the hell are you doing?' Now, it's so many Green Day fans' favorite record.'

Armstrong told *Rolling Stone:* After 'Time Of Your Life,' I started getting into playing more acoustic guitar, and I really wanted to have more for *Warning*. I had been listening to more of The Kinks and The Who, who found a lot of power in an acoustic song, and used the guitar almost like a drum. 'Pinball Wizard' is so percussive.'

But in hindsight, Billie Joe felt uneasy about *Warning*, telling *NME* in 2020:

I'd like to go back and re-record that album. It was right when Pro Tools started happening. I want to go back and just do everything more live, because I think 'Minority' live is a lot better than it came out on the album. But that's just one of those things that you think about too much. Those songs on *Warning,* I really wanted to flesh out. I think *Warning*'s the one right now that I look at that maybe at the time was sort of misunderstood.

'Warning' (Lyrics: Armstrong; Music: Green Day)

It's a new day and a new way for Green Day. 'Warning' opens their first 2000s album softer than any fan could ever have expected at the time. In the 1990s, the band had written approximately 100 songs, with at least 90% of them in the pop-punk vein, but they put down the aggression for a lot of *Warning.* Electric guitars are replaced with acoustics for the slogan-laden title track's crisp folk-rock verses. Mike is more prominently featured on backing vocals, like on *Dookie.* It was a great plan to go this softer route, erasing much of their personality to revamp their identity and start over. They're practicing what they're preaching by 'living without warning,' and thinking like individuals when they hit the market with one of the most unlikely sounds to come from a band associated with punk: folk rock. The pop hooks and melody are in full bloom, and there's no distortion to possibly disrupt them.

'Warning' is the third significant leap in Armstrong's lyric writing. It's the first world topic he's addressed on a serious level without having a tantrum since 'Road To Acceptance': a song that defended minorities. It's his first full-on universally-topical song that doesn't tie in with something else. The lyric priority was to dissect society without bringing in his own frustrations. He tells it from the first-person perspective, taking various terms from signage, slogans and general common expressions to create a warning to not live your life ruled by things that extinguish individualism.

Billie Joe begins the album with 'This is a public service announcement,' imitating 'Know Your Rights' – the famous opener of The Clash's *Combat Rock* (1982). We get 'may impair your ability to operate machinery,' 'Keep out of reach of children' and additional warnings. In verse two, he continues his new universal outlook, looking at 'safety-sealed communities,' asking, 'Is the cop or am I the one who's really dangerous?' Billie doesn't care about the answer but wants people to question the actions of the police. He expressed this to *Rolling Stone* in 2020:

I wrote this right before the election between George Bush and Al Gore. I think that song is sort of about declaring that you're stepping out of the line, you're not part of the sheep, and you're trying to find your own individualism. It felt like we were diving into something that was more conceptual for sure.

The video shows the band performing the song in a guy's kitchen. The guy gets up, gets dressed and heads to the pool then goes to work at a factory. He portrays the 'victim of authority.'

'Blood, Sex And Booze' (Lyrics: Armstrong; Music: Green Day)
Tré brings back the 'Hitchin' A Ride' rhythm here. While it's a bit odd sitting as the album's second song, the S&M mood doesn't throw it off course, and the band bring some of their typical hard-hitting muscularity. The break is surprisingly uneventful, as it could've been filled with some of the enjoyable sound effects used previously. It winds up more like a piledriving hard-rock song, getting faster as it moves but never feeling like punk. There's a lighter, tongue-in-cheek vibe.

The song might've been the sequel to 'Dominated Love Slave' from *Kerplunk*, but it's a totally different topic to the one from 'Warning.' Billie Joe has finally decided to tackle any subject, mix scenarios and play other characters throughout an album. He prays for dominatrix sex, blood and booze. The blood would come from the raunchy sex, while the booze continues the alcohol references: a major theme of *Nimrod* and its B-sides. It details the basics of his fun fictional relationship and his submission. It never gets graphic or violent; it's supposed to be humorous. The oddest and maybe most-graphic moment comes from the odd second verse: 'Mandolin of discipline/Throw me to the dogs/Let them eat my flesh down to the wood/It feels so good.'

'Church On Sunday' (Lyrics: Billie Armstrong; Music: Green Day)
The pop-punk is back, but it heavily favors the pop side, with less distortion, some creditable hooks and a splendid melody: part of which was brought back years later for 'The Static Age' on *21st Century Breakdown*. It's brisk, but more relaxed and loving than a lot of their 1990s material. The break brings in a few Townshend's windmill guitar swoops, before it tosses in one more killer chorus and a lightly Beatlesque ending.

The narrator apologizes in a relationship with a religious woman. The cute chorus, 'If I promise to go to church on Sunday/Will you go with me on Friday night?,' is then Armstrong-ized with his typical *melodramatic-fool* turn: 'If you live with me, I'll die for you and this compromise.' It's the kind of desperate line he used in his earliest love songs.

'Fashion Victim' (Lyrics: Billie Armstrong; Music: Green Day)
'Fashion Victim' finds Green Day casting their style aside, and trying on new clothing. Armstrong uses scratchy guitar and a lighter, bright rhythm, while popular veteran session musician Benmont Tench sings on the break.

The lyric addresses the cutthroat side of the fashion industry, with lines like, 'He's a casualty, dressed to the teeth in the latest genocide' bringing the melodrama and wordplay of *Nimrod* to a new topic. It's another third-person, topical lyric: like many on *Warning, revealing a* corporate fashion industry where surface is promoted over substance. 'What's in a name?,' Billie asks in the chorus as he thinks of all the big-name designers.

'Do the anorex-a-go-go/Cloaked with style for pedophiles' addresses two major issues with modelling. Armstrong blames everybody in the industry,

69

from the big-name designers and corporations, to the models themselves – and us: a society that often cares more about appearance than personality.

'Castaway' (Lyrics: Armstrong; Music: Green Day)

Green Day get funky for the fun 'Castaway.' Unlike the mostly acoustic title track, the rest of the album uses a mix of electric and acoustic guitars. Armstrong's vocal feels like a spirit flying high, excited at his new sonic discoveries. He sounds somewhat rejuvenated throughout the album, and this vocal brings a new playful side that fits with a lot of the highly-clever lyrics.

Billie Joe is getting so much better as a lyricist here. With 'Castaway,' the band are off, away from the pop-punk world, setting sail to classic rock and folk rock islands not usually explored by punk-driven bands. 'I'm on a sentimental journey into sight and sound of no return/And no looking back or down.' He sings, 'I'm on a mission into destination unknown/An expedition into Desolation Road.' In verse three, Billie Joe returns to the topic of taking chances, adding another 'spontaneous combustion' line from 'Bab's Uvula Who?' The breakdown is like a party on this entertaining island, with Billie Joe the happiest castaway out there. Ironically, exactly two months after 'Castaway' came out, the famous film of the same name starring Tom Hanks was released to much acclaim. Green Day's castaway seems a lot happier.

'Misery' (Green Day)

After the last few tunes combined the band's old and new styles, 'Misery' is a journey into the unknown. This cabaret-type tune also sounds happier than its lyric. As the character describes some pitfalls of life, his memories of Disney have him creating another interesting and odd atmosphere, that Green Day would never touch again. It has a late-night, after-dark feel. Usually, a Farfisa organ is for psychedelic effect as heard in the 1960s, but the one played by Mike here creates and almost circus-like vibe. Armstrong even adds some mandolin lines, before trumpets duel with that 1950s-type guitar line. It's one of the stranger moments of one of their most quirky and longest songs yet. It's their most intricate arrangement yet, and shows surprising growth.

Billie Joe creates a collection of short stories in a single song, as if he was Bob Dylan. On his song 'Desolation Row,' Dylan ends each character's story by having them wind up on desolation row. Here, Billie Joe has each character wind up in misery.

Virginia, the Floridian prostitute, 'hitched a ride to misery,' as if misery was a place. A second character – Mr. Whirly – ends up panhandling misery, unable to survive in San Francisco after liquidating his estate. He falls asleep on the Haight – the 1960s hippie hotspot which became rundown and filled with the homeless in the decades that followed. Vinnie the drug hustler from Amsterdam, gets killed the same night, and a character named Gina marries Virginia from verse one. The men die, and the women get married. It's a loose commentary on destiny, fate, actions, consequences, cause and effect. Like in real life, everyone's lives are simultaneously changing.

The first part of the chorus, 'We're gonna get high high high when we're low low low' could be based on Wings' 1972 hit 'Hi, Hi, Hi.' 'Misery' and The Who's 'A Quick One (While He's Away)' served as prototypes for *American Idiot*.

'Deadbeat Holiday' (Lyrics: Armstrong; Music: Green Day)

Though the throwback 'Deadbeat Holiday' starts with a stuttering effect, it's really a trip back home to Rodeo for the band. They start briefly with a mid-tempo rhythm before going back to their standard pop-punk sound. The tune borrows heavily from 'Nice Guys Finish Last,' with matching chorus melodies. The imaginative lines, 'Wake up/The house is on fire and the cat's in the dryer/Philosophy's a liar when your home's your headstone' was quoted several times in reviews as an effective way to set up a song.

Armstrong sings in the second person, as he usually does when he's on the attack – giving his assessment of someone who's lazy and apathetic. This deadbeat wakes up on his birthday to find that's he going to be burned alive. He's advised to pray for his life or enjoy his last moments. The dark humor here is that the narrator keeps reminding the deadbeat that at least he's not alone because he is with him – but he keeps picking on him.

'Hold On' (Lyrics: Armstrong; Music: Green Day)

Calling Bob Dylan! Billie Joe said *Warning* was influenced by Dylan's *Bringing It All Back Home*, and 'Hold On' has the most evidence that this was the case. It's led by acoustic guitars providing lyrical lines, and harmonica. The sweet melody is uplifting like the lyric, and the upbeat, cheery music helps balance out all their nasty-sounding songs of old. Though it sounds like Dylan's instrumentation, it comes closest to Beatles songs like 'Love Me Do,' 'Please Please Me' or 'I Should Have Known Better.' Because of its close resemblance to that song, Armstrong re-recorded the harmonica part, so it was less prominent.

'Hold On' starts with the terrific line, 'When I step to the edge on the shadow of a doubt', which shows the cloud cast over the protagonist. He's looking for a new start after living in a halfway house. In an interview Billie Joe did with Alan DiPerna for *Guitar World*, he said, 'That song was about a friend of mine who had three friends die within one year.'

'Jackass' (Lyrics: Armstrong; Music: Green Day)

A standard pop-punk rhythm gets swept up by saxophone from guest player Doug Meek. This time the target is a guy who clowns around a lot, using stale jokes that get tiresome after a while. Armstrong was an ace at not using the same axiom or adage, and he brings one altered expression in: 'To know you is to hate you.'

'Waiting' (Lyrics: Armstrong; Music: Green Day)

The heavenly melody here bursts in like the sun brightening the lives of everyone it touches. Easily the album's strongest melody, and their sweetest-ever this side of 'Good Riddance,' 'Waiting' was a big hit, and deservedly so. It's punchy and aggressive but uplifting; inspirational but not overly giddy. It breaks down to acoustic guitar for a quiet bridge but otherwise is energetic. It starts with the stellar chorus with only Billie Joe on vocal and guitar, then the band swoop in with an appropriately-light sound, only darkening on the buildups to the chorus and bridge. Armstrong finally provides the lighter, brighter, jangle *Dookie*-style breaks that had been sorely missing.

By 2000, Green Day knew they were an inspiration and consolation to millions of fans, who listened to Billie Joe's troubles or fictional troubles, and could commiserate with them. Sensing this, Armstrong began writing more uplifting, motivational songs, and 'Waiting' qualifies as one.

Before a concert, Billie Joe is waiting in the wings, ready to put on the show of his life. But it could easily be a Green Day fan getting ready for their own moment in the sun, like a speech, a marriage, a promotion or a new baby, and they're nervous in anticipation. It's a song that can fit any event and anybody. It's universal, which makes it one of the band's best songs. 'Downtown lights will be shining on me,' he sings, referencing how many cities are set up, so their downtown sections are the most populated, and the melody's inspiration from the 1960s Petula Clark hit 'Downtown.' One line goes, 'Go downtown where all the lights are bright.' Billie Joe explained to Larry Livermore in 2009: 'It's about putting your best foot forward, even if you don't have any idea what's in store for the future; about trying to make a difference in your own life; about having high goals even though you're not fully sure of what you want or where you're going to end up. You just keep moving forward and don't give up.'

'Minority' (Lyrics: Armstrong; Music: Green Day)

Like 'Waiting', 'Minority' has a short acoustic intro before diving into another song that matches rollicking, militant rhythms with a sweet vocal melody and massive hooks strong enough to lift a person's spirit. It's the album's most enduring track and its biggest hit. Who would've thought a band like Green Day could sneak in a harmonica break, sing merrily and still come up with one of their biggest numbers.

'Minority' is about being an individual and not listening to politician's slogans and warnings. It's the song that catapulted the band's ambitions towards *American Idiot*. Billie Joe told *Rolling Stone* in 2020: 'I started feeling the political wheels starting to turn toward conservatism a little bit. I think that song is sort of about declaring that you're stepping out of the line, you're not part of the sheep, and trying to find your own individualism. It felt like we were diving into something that was more conceptual for sure.'

The song references a religious right-wing conservative group that began in the 1970s. 'I pledge allegiance to the underworld,' he sneakily sings, changing the original expression from 'I pledge allegiance to the United States of America,' equating the country to an underworld. 'One nation under dog,' he sarcastically sings, taking 'God' and reversing it to metaphorically notify us that the country thinks backwards. Billie Joe figured it would be a nice insult if Republican candidate George W. Bush got elected, making him the 'dog' the nation's under. He also created a double entendre from the other side by taking the word 'underdog' and turning it into an insult.

The singer breaks out of the mold, and leaves the herd of sheep, marching to his own beat. 'One light, one mind, flashing in the dark.' He ends verse two with the excellent motivational line, 'You are your own sight.'

'Macy's Day Parade' (Lyrics: Armstrong; Music: Green Day)

Every Thanksgiving in New York City, the Macy's Day Parade takes place, and people from around the US watch huge kid-themed celebrity balloon floats and performers doing a variety of acts. World-famous department store Macy's initiated the parade in 1924. It's usually a fun time for all, and the next day – like many stores – Macy's give Black Friday discounts. Billie Joe feels that this is the commercialization of a holiday that was not meant to celebrate shopping.

He sings the song in a deeper, tired voice as he used on 'Rest,' and though it's clear he's down, when he sings of hope, he sounds like he has hope. This emotional dichotomy is the first time he tried to vary his singing style in song. David Campbell's beautiful string arrangement brings as much to this song as the one on 'Good Riddance (Time Of Your Life),' and gives a welcome break to the perhaps slightly-harsh acoustic guitars.

It's clear that the opening couplet 'Today's the Macy's Day Parade/The night of the living dead is on its way' has Billie comparing the zombie sheep of 'Minority' that are stampeding on one another to get the best deal, to the 1968 horror flick *Night of the Living Dead*. Armstrong's facetious sense of humor, rises to the forefront on lines like, 'Stuffed in a coffin/ Ten per cent more free,' 'Red-light special at the mausoleum,' and the chorus line 'Economy-sized dreams of hope.' The anti-materialist attitude is detailed throughout the song. Billie Joe wanted all the toys when he was a kid, but grew out of that need to have everything, and instead – as he so sweetly sings – "Cause I'm thinking 'bout a brand new hope/The one I've never known/'Cause now I know that it's all that I wanted.' The pessimist throughout the 1990s is in a new decade and a new century. And like so many others at the turn of the millennium, he wanted a fresh start for an improved life: which links back to 'Waiting.' He offered thoughts on the tune to *Blue Railroad* in 2009: 'Macho brutality doesn't necessarily mean you're a good songwriter. I think that some Beatles songs are way more punk rock than most punk songs written today.'

Ironically, years later, when *American Idiot* made it to Broadway, the cast played and sang 'Good Riddance (Time Of Your Life)' at the Macy's Day Parade.

Related tracks
'Outsider' (Dee Dee Ramone)
Though this sing-songy Ramones cover is played keeping things simple and raw, the surprisingly-strong melody is allowed space to breathe, and the track comes off as one of Green Day's better early classic rock covers. The band enliven all the hooks of The Ramones' 1983 song. Like much alternative-rock subject matter, the song is about feeling like an outsider or being cast as one by general society. The band are as tight and crisp as ever, occasionally intercut with Armstrong's deep guitar tone. They sing the bridge as a group moment of camaraderie.

'Scumbag' (Lyrics: Dirnt; Music: Green Day)
'Scumbag' is a sneakily-fine tune since its effective, optimistic melody matches the scumbag that thinks he can improve his situation before Billie Joe shuts him down. By the time Green Day fans heard 'Scumbag,' it was clear Billie Joe could write attack songs in his sleep, and was perhaps on automatic with this B-side. 'You're clothes look different, but you're still the same' he spits at the scumbag who perhaps had a change of class. Billie Joe hates him and thinks the friendless scumbag visited him for favors.

'Maria' (Lyrics: Armstrong; Music: Green Day)
The speedy 'Maria' is a fun song, and its happy-spirited, bright presentation finds Tré particularly inspired through the breakdowns and multiple parts. There's extra kick compared to some of the more tired efforts on the latter half of *Nimrod:* the album that's closest to this track's sound. Dirnt leads the verses rhythmically without Armstrong's guitar around, and Tré drives the song home with an adrenaline rush before its abrupt conclusion.

'Maria' could be 'Whatsername' from *American Idiot,* in disguise. Maria is a rebel, who 'smashed the radio with the board of education.' 'Burning the flag at half mast/She's the rebel's forgotten son,' Billie Joe sings, like he's thinking of Amanda. The line 'She'll drag the weights to keep the vendetta alive,' predicts how 'Whatsername' served as an inspiration for the lead character of *American Idiot:* the Jesus of Suburbia. 'Turned up the static left of the state of the nation' is a political dig using static to represent the noise or nonsense spewed out by certain politicians and the lack of forward movement as a nation.

It anticipates 'The Static Age' from *21st Century Breakdown* by almost a decade. It's a 'Waiting' B-side that wound up as the opening track on *International Superhits!*

'I Don't Want To Know If You Are Lonely' (Grant Hart)

Husker Du's *Candy Apple Grey* (1986) held the original version of this song that tied in with Green Day's jaded-love conquest attempts. Many thought Husker Du were a major influence on early Green Day, and it's proven with this very rare track. One of their least-known releases, it's not too shabby since the band knows how to cradle the melody in a sea of grumbling bass and cymbal hits. Armstrong lets the rhythm section do most of the work, feeding it seldomly as it speeds along. Surprisingly, the band don't sound as comfortable as they do on their other cover songs. There's an unofficial YouTube video from MTV 2 with the band performing the song in the studio, with a bit of original Husker Du footage. It's a 2000 B-side found on the 'Warning' single. This song was eventually reissued as a bonus track on 2009's *The Green Day Collection*.

International Superhits! (Compilation) (2001)

This was the band's first greatest hits record and included the B-side 'Maria' and the previously-unreleased song 'Poprocks And Coke'. 'J.A.R.' appears for the first time on a Green Day album.

'Poprocks And Coke' (Lyrics: Armstrong; Music: Green Day)

This relaxed and reliable track is one of Green Day's poppiest numbers. But it's not quite hit material, and sitting on *International Superhits!*, it's lucky it comes before those biggies, because this is nowhere near greatest-hits level. It's a friendly song about being there for someone else.

Shenanigans (Compilation) (2002)

This B-side collection included one new song.

'Ha Ha You're Dead' (Lyrics: Dirnt; Music: Green Day)

With bass-and-drums-only on the verses, Billie Joe's evil attack is heard loud and clear. The hostility comes to the forefront as the group sings the song title over a recycled sing-along chorus melody with guitar thrashing away. After he briefly steps off the gas with a hard-edged jangly guitar break, he comes back for the final verse and chorus, overlapping it with the original guitar riff.

Probably Green Day's most evil song, Mike Dirnt wrote the distasteful lyric as a wicked tribute to Tim Yohannan: the Gilman owner, who'd died from cancer a couple of years earlier. It's a low blow, and despite the band conducting many attacks that were based partially or wholly on real people, this couldn't be more distasteful unless they sung Tim's name. It's an unfair kicking of a man when he's permanently down, and for a band who did millions good and few harm, besides 'Platypus', it's Green Day's ugliest moment.

'I Fought The Law' (Sonny Curtis)

This is a conventional attempt at the Sonny Curtis song, with a sweet
instrumental break of Armstrong's chorus-pedal guitar effect singing over a
complicated stop/start rhythmic portion: one of Dirnt and Tré's more-creative
moments. It's an impassioned delivery by the band, who rock the song harder
than The Clash, and perhaps just as effectively. The great original hooks are
loud and clear through the heavy distortion.

American Idiot (2004)

Personnel:
Billie Joe Armstrong: lead vocals, guitar, piano
Mike Dirnt: bass, backing vocals; lead vocals ('Nobody Likes You'),
'Homecoming' (Partial)
Tré Cool: drums, percussion, backing vocals; lead vocal ('Rock And Roll
Girlfriend': part of 'Homecoming')
Rob Cavallo: piano
Jason Freese: saxophone
Kathleen Hanna: vocals ('Letterbomb')
Producers: Rob Cavallo, Green Day
Recorded at Studio 880, Oakland, CA; Ocean Way Studio B, Hollywood; Capitol,
Hollywood
Label: Reprise
Release date: 21 September 2004
Charts: US: 1, UK: 1
Singles: 'American Idiot,' 'Boulevard Of Broken Dreams,' 'Holiday,' 'Wake Me Up
When September Ends,' 'Jesus Of Suburbia'

It had been four years since the last album, and the band felt like they
needed a change of sound. Their popularity dipped some after *Warning,* with
pop-punk less prominent on radio. They came up with the idea of a rock
opera, of all things. Their big influence The Who remained relevant, and they
followed in their footsteps. The Who had two famous rock operas – *Tommy*
(1969) and *Quadrophenia* (1973). But it was their 1966 ten-minute mini rock
opera 'A Quick One, While He's Away' that served as the direct inspiration for
American Idiot.

There are three main characters. The stifled Jesus of Suburbia wants to
break free of conformity, think for himself and lead people to a mental place
where they think for themselves. The second character St. Jimmy is the first
character's alter ego. St. Jimmy wants to party all night long because he's
given up hope on making the country a better place. The third character is
Whatsername – a woman who thinks for herself, doesn't conform and has a
philosophy that agrees with the Jesus of Suburbia.

In a way, the Jesus of Suburbia is similar to Billie Joe's past protagonists from
albums like *39/Smooth, Kerplunk,* and some from *Dookie* who questioned
themselves and thought of an uncertain future, wallowing in the bedroom
of teenage angst and heartbreak. St. Jimmy recalls characters on albums like
Insomniac and *Nimrod* who let loose their anger and frustration against society
because they'd given up hope, concentrating on selfish means like partying
hard, drinking, spewing hate and seeking revenge. Whatsername is like Billie
Joe's romantic, sympathetic and honest characters from his earliest love songs.

Green Day were all for taking the political route and playing music about
the world around them. It wasn't just Billie Joe – Mike and Tré were ready as

well. Tre mentioned their new world views on VH1 *Storytellers*: 'The escalated censorship lately: what are you gonna do? – lay down and roll over and be saved and put something out that won't have anything about being saved, or are you gonna stick your neck out?; they can bleep out what they want to bleep out – and say what's supposed to be said. That's Green Day style.'

Mike added, 'The different structures on this record that we really wanted to go for – if we're writing about characters, then I think a lot of the highs and lows and the structural shifts of gear and stuff has to be like real life; it has to really affect you. People say rock 'n' roll can change things. If it just changes the mind of someone for a second, then yes, it can change things.'

The band were still highly creative on *Warning*, but with poor sales, many thought they were done. Armstrong was still in his songwriting prime – in fact, at a peak.

American Idiot may be the band's greatest set of compositions. Some say it's their best album, and the experiment was a massive success. It eventually sold 16,000,000 and became maybe the last important rock album with cultural impact. It had a heavy impact on a whole new generation of youth, and brought Green Day massive fame.

The band's clean slate was evident in the exceptional song arrangements and outstanding dynamics and new tricks. But the album's drama and importance come from the band's unbelievable interplay, willingness to extend past three-minute songs, and the best lyrics Billie Joe had ever written. They expand their sound at length in exciting musical ideas.

'American Idiot' (Lyrics: Armstrong; Music: Green Day)

The moment Armstrong's guitar bursts out of the speakers, *American Idiot* feels like a roller-coaster ride towards the edge of the world or the end of the world: it's too hard to tell, since everything feels like a blur. 'American Idiot' is a dizzying, turbocharged delight that was their best hard-rock song in quite some time. The primary guitar figure is outstanding, and the production has grown to stadium proportions. Armstrong lets loose on the guitar break with a call-to-arms arena-rock tone that's frentic, sharp and brutal.

The song opens the album, similar to how 'Warning' opened *Warning*. Both opening title tracks strove for individualism. 'Warning' is about not living life by slogan guidance, while 'American Idiot' is about propaganda, media, and government's effect on individuals' lives, and how only an American idiot would believe everything they read. Though it has an anti-George W. Bush sentiment, the 'idiot' represents the person who blindly eats up whatever they're fed by organizations with selfish motives. Armstrong doesn't want to be an American idiot, and he sings the song as if he's addressing the nation from a podium.

'Welcome to a new kind of tension all across the alienation' has Billie Joe at his best lyrically. He's come a long way from his early romance/frustration days. Now he can manipulate words, phrases and their moods on a level that competes with almost any songwriter of the era. He sounds celebratory by adding 'Welcome,' and on other lines like 'Now everybody do the propaganda/And sing along to the age of paranoia,' like he's a host of hell, instructing people on how to do the newest dance. 'One nation controlled by the media/Information age of hysteria/It's calling out to idiot America,' he sings, blaming the media for causing additional hysteria: particularly after 9/11. Billie Joe told NPR in 2010:

> In every song I write – whether it's a love song or a political song or a song about family – the one thing that I find, is feeling lost and trying to find your way. I think 'American Idiot' is a series of questions. I think 'Holiday' is a series of questions. It's like, you're trying to battle your way out of your own ignorance, like, 'I don't want to be an American idiot. What I want to be, I'm not sure, but I just want more, and I'm willing to take the risk to try to get out of that.

Billie Joe told MTV:

> I think, politically, 'American Idiot' when we were writing it, it was trying to make sense out of a big mess. You're trying to find something to believe in, but it's difficult when you're getting bombarded with useless information. So it's just trying to find your identity and your individualism in the midst of all that.

'Jesus of Suburbia' (Lyrics: Armstrong; Music: Green Day)
This is the centerpiece of *American Idiot*, where the band ascend to full-blown ambition levels by signaling the beginning of the story arc. Perhaps their most complex and ambitious song, the band-and-fan favorite suite is split into five parts.

'Jesus Of Suburbia – I: Jesus Of Suburbia'
This incredible track may be the crowning epic of all Green Day epics, and as it plays for over nine minutes, it's clear they had never been this ambitious. The beautiful opening section is overstuffed with emotional vocals and logically-powerful transitions, never sounding forced. Billie Joe liked the contrast of rage and love, and later in the album, he sings 'Heart like a hand grenade' – another way of providing the same contrast. He's also singing in the first-person like he typically did on songs both personal and topical. But this time, he the voice and puppeteer of a character that continues to exist as the album continues. Billie Joe continues to sing on behalf of various characters – for the most part – from here on out.

As the Jesus of Suburbia, Billie Joe sings about his typical day, revealing his personality aspects. 'The bible of none of the above' describes him as agnostic or non-religious. By verse two, he's watching television. His confidence cracks, and he turns to drugs, the excellent songwriting continuing with the line, 'To fall in love and fall in debt/With alcohol and cigarettes and Mary Jane.' The Jesus of Suburbia feels like nobody is looking out for him. The band are at the top of their game during the chorus, capped off with the excellent line, 'In a land of make-believe that don't believe in me'.

'Jesus Of Suburbia – II: The City Of The Damned'
In the second part continues Armstrong's love of slogans and mottos.

> The motto was just a lie
> It said, 'Home is where the heart is'
> But what a shame, 'cause everybody's heart doesn't beat the same
> It's beating out of time

He doesn't feel like he has a sanctuary in the world. The melody is first-rate, and the overall track is dynamic and adventurous, leaving the listener unclear about which way the band will go. We go back to the broken-down wasteland of 'Welcome To Paradise,' as Billie Joe sings of a hopeless mini-society living in an anonymous suburb that's given up on its citizens.

'Jesus Of Suburbia – III: I Don't Care'
Billie Joe goes on a roaring tirade for an apathetic chorus that rounds up the millions of bored teenagers in suburbs around the country so that together they can strive for something more than their boring cookie-cutter lives. The band's brash and violent assault continues, but they remain brainy.

'Jesus Of Suburbia – IV: Dearly Beloved'
Calming down the fiery rock with some melodic cool water and reflective moments, the listener gets a breather here. It's only a brief relief, before the stress kicks in and the band continues down their war-torn aural path. Billie Joe reaches back to his childhood, teen years and early confusion-soaked songs, to ask, 'Are we demented or am I disturbed?/The space that's between insane and insecure.' Going against the grain, feeds the Jesus of Suburbia's feelings of oppression.

'Jesus Of Suburbia – V: Tales Of Another Broken Home'
Tré absolutely crushes the drums here, somehow upping the ante with his greatest performance yet. His exquisite timing leads to some excellent dramatic dynamics. There's a beautiful piano moment before the band bring it home for one final anthemic chorus.

The subtitle 'Tales Of A Broken Home' speaks for itself. In 2004, everyone knew the US divorce rate was 51%, therefore, there were more broken homes. The Jesus of Suburbia runs away, losing faith in his small town. Billie Joe likened it to his own youth when he spoke to NPR: 'Try to get out and see something more, and, you know, for me, I had a place called Gilman Street, and it was a club, a punk-rock club in Berkeley, and I was just introduced to a lot of new ideas. I think that was my escape.'

He also discussed it with *Rolling Stone*:

I loved *A Quick One* by The Who, and I decided I'd love to write a song that felt like a mini-opera. We had a studio that we could work everything out at and experiment, and Mike, Tré and I had been coming up with little 30-second vignettes, and tried to connect them in the studio. After I wrote 'American Idiot,' I was like, 'Who is this character?' Then the ideas started firing at me – I'm the son of rage and love, the Jesus of Suburbia, the bible of none of the above.

'Holiday' (Lyrics: Armstrong; Music: Green Day)

'Holiday' was Green Day's first anti-war, anti-violence statement, as politics had been a low priority for the band for much of the 1990s. *Warning* awoke a new 21st-century Green Day, ready to tackle the world and all its headaches. But *American Idiot* was on a grander scale, something that was written as a major statement, with intricacy and complexity beyond what they'd done before.

The militant rhythm and *Warning*-like arrangement soaked in loud distorted guitar always propels the fantastic melody and hooks. Billie Joe's guitar sounds are laid between the downbeats in such an organized way that it's like he's putting his socks perfectly into his drawer for room inspection.

As the soldiers fall, Billie facetiously requests another call for a fictious song. This time, he wants soldiers to sing 'Faith And Misery,' but it's really just a part of the narrative. He switches to the Jesus of Suburbia character for the chorus. He's aware of the trappings in his surroundings now he's broken free from the city of the damned: 'I beg to dream and differ from the hollow lies/ This is the dawning of the rest of our lives/On holiday. 'Billie Joe told MTV: 'I am anti-war, so a lot of it has to do with that, and there's different sides of it too. Like, there's one line that sort of messes with liberals a little too, where it says, 'Hear the drums pounding out of time/Another protester has crossed the line/To find the money's on the other side.'

His brilliant songwriting continues to shine on lines like, 'Can I get another 'Amen'?/There's a flag wrapped around a score of men/A gag, a plastic bag on a monument,' signifying the religious ties entwined with the Iraq war and the tight mental hold he felt the US government had on its citizens. It makes sense that the bridge that follows is a speech from the 'representative of California,' and of course, it's played by Billie Joe, who speaks for conformity and threatens those who step out of line. He told *Rolling Stone*:

That was a time when our country was moving into a war for fictitious reasons. A lot of it had to do with politics and oil. It felt like the country was beginning to come apart. I think the catalyst of where we're at now really is with George W. Bush. So this song was just about trying to find your own voice and your own individuality, and questioning everything that you see on television, in politics, school, family and religion. I was jumping into character a little bit. I wanted something that sounded very nasty. I definitely wanted to do something that was provocative. So I was like, 'Sieg Heil to the president Gasman,' invoking old Nazi-Germany propaganda films, contrasted with the American branches of government. I was just kind of messing around and using the English language against itself. With the riff, I was messing around with chords in a different way, and putting in some echo and delay on it, doing what I normally do and trying to come up with riffs.

'Boulevard Of Broken Dreams' (Lyrics: Armstrong; Music: Green Day)

Known as Green Day's best or second-best ballad, 'Boulevard Of Broken Dreams' is the ultimate walking song. If there were driving songs, there could be walking songs, and with its 'I walk alone' chorus (a bit reminiscent of Johnny Cash's 'I Walk The Line'), it's a song every loner can get with. The incredible melody can hit anybody anywhere at any time, and it will be effective. The tremolo-effect sound mixed with sparse rhythm guitar is the most unique Green Day sound yet. Armstrong's voice is resonant and emotionally enriched, as he works out the highs and lows of life. He explained the song title on *VH1 Storytellers*: 'There's an old James Dean photo where he's walking in New York, and underneath, it said, 'Boulevard of broken dreams.' It's a real place in my heart, man!'

Mr. Jesus of Suburbia had been calling his compatriots to action on declaring he didn't want to be an 'American idiot,' and calling for a new dawning on 'Holiday', but he's one of many sheep who have eaten what they've been fed and are now content to not have the added hassle of helping others, so he feels lonely in his revolution. He's realizing it's one thing to call for action, and another to convince others to actually *take* action. He goes against the grain, and wonders why the grain has not turned in his favor.

Armstrong makes sure to mention that the Jesus of Suburbia feels like he's home on a lonely road because it's his metaphor for feeling alone in his thinking relative to others around him. Past Green Day protagonists were going to stay home and wallow, but Jesus goes out and roams late at night.

'Are We The Waiting' (Lyrics: Armstrong: Music: Green Day)

This song has a 1970s Broadway-style chorus, and brilliant chord changes that can rip a heart out of a chest. The band tug and play with their listeners' brains, ears and hearts throughout *American Idiot* and do it on such a large scale that the ambition is staggering. The huge chorus sounds like a community singing. Billie Joe told *Storytellers*: 'I was walking around on a misty night in New York City, and I think it's a point in the record where the character is on the verge of losing his mind. He's very vulnerable and it's right before St. Jimmy comes up.'

'Are We the Waiting' continues the lonely late-night walk of a distraught Jesus of Suburbia, wondering when there will come a time when people stand up and fight for their rights. But for now, he's resigned to think, 'The rage and love, the story of my life/The Jesus of Suburbia is a lie,' because he failed to lead people closer to their best lives, free of control. His enthusiasm feels dumb in hindsight. Disappointed with his thoughts of breaking free from his confining hometown and living a happy life, he discards this personality and takes on one that says, 'Screw it all, let's party!' The line, 'Heads or tails, fairy tales in my mind', somehow links the two sides of a coin.

'St. Jimmy' (Lyrics: Armstrong: Music: Green Day)

The hard-core 'St. Jimmy' is one of Green Day's fastest songs, seeking speed levels like 'Platypus,' is almost in 'Take Back' territory, and it's blazing fury blasts like lightning. It's full-throttle in rhythm and full-throated vocally, Billie Joe introducing himself as the devilish St. Jimmy: the alter ego of the Jesus of Suburbia. He's given up on trying to make change for good and just wants to live it up apathetically. By the time he introduces himself, he's a small-time criminal smoker with a heroin habit, who thinks he's so self-destructive, he can be viewed as suicidal. As Jimmy, Billie Joe sings, 'Raised in the city in a halo of lights/Product of war and fear that we've been victimized.' Amongst his self-identifiers is 'King of Forty Thieves': a play on the old folk tale 'Ali Baba And The Forty Thieves' from the *One Thousand and One Nights* collection. Jimmy quips he's 'A son of a bitch and Edgar Allen Poe,' facetiously representing his nasty, hurtful side and his dark, brooding side. This excellent thrasher finds Jimmy at his worst, lending murderous intent to his gun threats. Billie Joe explained the song to *Storytellers:* 'The original thought was that (St. Jimmy and Jesus of Suburbia) were the same person. It could be two different people. I love St. Jimmy, he's pretty cool and he's pretty sexy, but he's part of a split personality. They just get disconnected from themselves and follow a self-destructive path, and I think St. Jimmy sort of symbolizes that.'

'Give Me Novocaine' (Lyrics: Armstrong; Music: Green Day)

This song starts with a bit of the big beat from 'Are We the Waiting,' and ends up sounding like a grungy version of 'St. Jimmy.' Its beautifully somber opening contrasts well with its loud and uncompromising guitar riffs and stop/start rhythm.

Billie Joe reaches back to *Insomniac*, with physically-ailing lyrics. He addresses Novocaine; he's so relieved that he has it; asking the drug to give him a 'long kiss goodnight.' While *Insomniac* also focused on the body failing, the drug way of coping was barely mentioned. *Nimrod* found the band frequently self-medicating with alcohol. It's not far from original punk's drug-tale songs. He told NPR: 'I think 'Novocaine' is a song about trying to find that escape in places that are probably not the most healthy things in the world. If you let it take you over and really lose yourself in it, I think that 'Novocaine' is about a defining moment where you actually lose yourself into your own demons.'

'She's A Rebel' (Lyrics: Armstrong; Music: Green Day)

While more powerful than most of the tracks here, 'She's A Rebel' has a bright edge, like a ray of sunshine through the novocaine and clouds. The stop/start rhythm had been done, but this is one of the band's most cerebral assaults. They start with the chorus, direct and to the point, just like the rebel Whatsername: the female revolutionary who joins the cast of characters. 'She's a symbol of resistance and she's holding on my heart like a hand grenade' is the line that matches the album cover.

The song runs parallel to Billie Joe's experience dating Amanda – the inspiration for 'Chump,' 'She' and 'Sassafras Roots.' In some ways, he based Whatsername on her. Bikini Kill singer Kathleen Hanna was another woman he thought of, asking her to appear on the track 'Letterbomb.' Bikini Kill's 'Rebel Girl' is probably the musical centerpiece of the 1990s riot grrrl movement.

'Extraordinary Girl' (Lyrics: Armstrong; Music: Green Day)

The exotic rock of 'Extraordinary Girl' was the type of experimentation heard on *Warning* and is just as effective here. Armstrong tries different chords, and his hard jangling finds India, reminding us of some 1960s psychedelic excursions, but sounds closer to 1990s British band Kula Shaker. But the track's closest relative is The Yardbirds' 'Shapes Of Things,' which the melody of 'Extraordinary Girl' is based on.

If 'She's A Rebel' introduced and profiled Whatsername to the audience, then 'Extraordinary Girl' told the tale of how Jesus couldn't get up the nerve to ask out Whatsername – like the band's earliest protagonists. As an all-knowing narrator, he tells how both characters suffer. She cries at night over the way the world is, and tries to change it during the day. Jesus 'lacks the courage in his mind/Like a child left behind/Like a pet left in the rain,' just like Billie Joe's romantic characters of yesterday.

On *VH1 Storytellers*, Billie Joe praised Whatsername: 'I think the hero of the whole record was the Whatsername character. She's a person that never really wanes, falls from grace. She's the one who stuck to her beliefs and left all the bullshit behind.'

'Letterbomb' (Lyrics: Armstrong; Music: Green Day)

The adrenaline-loaded and theatrical 'Letterbomb' reveals how Cavallo's production and Green Day's playing are incredibly inspired. They come across as bigger and better than ever. Dirnt always knows when to punctuate the melody and rhythm. Vocally, Billie Joe continues to give it his all. With the help of riot grrrl legend Kathleen Hanna, the story progresses significantly. Though Billie Joe's ex-girlfriend Amanda was the inspiration for Whatsername, Hanna is a little easier to relate to since she's a rock star who's often the focus of documentaries, films and books. She encapsulates the *American Idiot* hero.

Whatsername gives Jesus a proper talking to, tossing some emotional-bombshell opinions into a letter addressed to him. 'Letterbomb' starts with a little nursery rhyme that ties in to the 'Nobody Likes You' segment that arrives during the 'Homecoming' suite. 'Letterbomb' is a vicious attack about Jesus being an 'American idiot' and 'going along for the ride' without really knowing what freedoms he's fighting for.

'The dummy failed the crash test, collecting unemployment checks' references the crash test dummies in 1990s US commercials for government initiatives to buckle your seatbelt. Jesus has crashed and burned and is unemployed, living off the government that he wanted to rebel against. Jesus hesitates to rebel fully since he feels alone in the fight. The chorus informs us that the 'city's burning' and Whatsername wants Jesus to take action now before it's too late. 'Where have all the bastards gone?' refers to those who are willing to go against the grain, but it also could be a play on the 1998 pop/rock hit by Paula Cole 'Where Have All the Cowboys Gone?'

As Jesus is reading the letter, by the second pre-chorus, Billie Joe assumes the voice in his head, switching out of second-person. He's fed up with his own *Quadrophenia*-like turns of personality. 'You're not the Jesus of Suburbia/The St. Jimmy is a figment of your mother's love/And your father's rage made me the idiot of America,' he sings, in his peak self-realization that these characters are just delusions of his true self and that he's more a balance of the two characters – and from his parents' influence, a balance of rage and love.

Because Billie Joe changed who is speaking in the song, it's safe to say Whatsername sings the first uplifting chorus, and Jesus sings it the second time around. He agrees with her that it's not too late to fight back unless it feels too much like a burden. If improving society with revolution is too much, then leave. The letter ends with Whatsername declaring that she's leaving their joint fight. She's also moving away, sensing that Jesus' political movement against the city is improbable and that the city's so bad that it's no longer livable. Armstrong explained in *Broadway Idiot*, the 2013 documentary about *American Idiot* on Broadway: 'Whatsername tells Jesus and St. Jimmy what he doesn't want to hear, but ultimately that's what they were going for, to begin with. That's the twist of the whole thing.'

'Wake Me Up When September Ends' (Lyrics: Armstrong; Music: Green Day)

Billie Joe's voice is on full display here, and he's more resonant than ever. His heart is out of his chest; he feels so close and personal. Riding a beautiful melody, he unravels a lovely profile filled with love and respect. The band kick it up a notch halfway through, with louder chiming guitars taking over alongside meaty beats and chugging bass. The band play with loud and soft dynamics until the end, when the song is allowed to sleep after one final enormous chorus hook.

'If there's one song that veers away from the story of the album, it's that one. It's just a personal thing. I never really tackled this issue – singing about my father or anything like that. It's hard to sing, but definitely therapeutic.' Billie Joe's father passed away when he was young, and he didn't get along well with his stepfather when his mother remarried. This song is all about his real father. He died in the month of September in 1982. Because of the album's political ties, many took the most personal song on *American Idiot*, and used it for their own grief, thinking of 9/11 victims and their loved ones. Each September, Billie Joe had to excruciatingly drag himself through dusty childhood memories of his father for the month. He just wants the month to end, so he doesn't have to suffer from the pain of his loss.

Billie Joe's jukebox always plays in his head when he writes lyrics. The song's chorus starts with the line 'Here comes the rain again,' reminding music fans of The Eurythmics' 1983 song of that title: another song that equates rain with reflection and sorrow.

Overall, the lyric is straightforward, resonant, emotional and clear – Billie Joe misses his father and remembers him well.

'Homecoming' (Lyrics: Armstrong; Music: Green Day); 'Nobody Likes You' section: (Dirnt); 'Rock And Roll Girlfriend' section: (Cool)

'Homecoming' was the song that inspired the *American Idiot* project. It upped Green Day's ambition to a point where it can be seen as the song they grew their sound with the most. The Who comparisons are obvious, since they are the most popular rock entity to attempt rock operas. 'Homecoming' is like *Tommy*'s 'We're Not Gonna Take It' – a long anthem that has catchy choruses everywhere and sums up the storyline, reaching a conclusion.

'Homecoming – 1: The Death Of St. Jimmy'

The vocal here is wrapped in a dirty filter, like it's coming from a tiny transistor radio and all this took place a century ago. With a Who-like chord progression, the band follows suit, occasionally pausing for small cause-and-effect sections.

Jesus' jolting and revolting alter ego St. Jimmy has taken the bullet. Realizing what Whatsername told him, Jesus ends his St. Jimmy personality. Jesus lost his dreams in the September rain in verse one – Billie Joe's way of linking the personal reflection of 'Wake Me Up When September Ends' with the Jesus of Suburbia character. The rain represents the end of Jesus and St. Jimmy's dreams of fame. 'There's no signs of hope/The stem and seeds of the last of the dope,' concludes St. Jimmy – a rare time Billie Joe uses a marijuana metaphor. St. Jimmy's pot is running out, just like his time partying and the stems and seeds. Annoyances when rolling a joint, represent the annoyances of living a party life. With some strong language of a figurative suicide, St. Jimmy is no more.

'Homecoming – 2: East 12th Street'

The album's best transition takes place at the beginning of this track – a transcendent moment that reaffirms Green Day can be unpredictable and exciting. It starts visceral and raw before working-in some pop.

Billie Joe here takes a police station he remembered being taken to during one of his real-life St. Jimmy moments, and used it as a subtitle for a song about apathy towards the dire situation of life in America that was all around him. Both characters are worn out. Whatsername left the town, and Jesus has been arrested. He's filling out paperwork so he can get out of jail. Forget trying to save a city.

'Homecoming – 3: Nobody Likes You'

This is Mike Dirnt's vocal moment in the spotlight. He uses the melody of 'Ring Around The Rosie' to taunt his target. It's one of the band's slowest moments, but it's a time to rest, as 'Homecoming' is over nine minutes long. His gives the update that Jesus is pining for Whatsername in the same way early Green Day characters longed for possible loves. This character falls asleep watching Spike TV: a network popular with youth in the 2000s. He drinks ten cups of coffee waiting for Whatsername, but to his dismay, she never shows. The 'Nobody likes you' chorus from 'Letterbomb' runs laps around his mind.

'Homecoming – 4: Rock And Roll Girlfriend'

The band snap out of the brief daze with Tré's contribution – a brief blast of fierce pop punk sung by the drummer himself. He hadn't sung a lead vocal since *Kerplunk* but doesn't sound like he minds dumping out his dirty laundry. It's a fun song that tries to look at the bright side of dating around the time of Tré's real-life divorce.

'Homecoming – 5: We're Coming Home Again'

The most massive-sounding chorus has arrived. It's the big *American Idiot* finale, except for the encore 'Whatsername.' It's bold and boisterous, it's made for Broadway, and would one day be performed on Broadway. This grandiose 'Homecoming' finale has cinematic musicality far beyond typical Green Day. Jesus and others are 'coming back from the edge of town' as if they tried and failed to change society for the better and are now coming home. It also could serve as a sly reference to Bruce Springsteen's *Darkness on the Edge of Town*.

There's a defeatist mentality that matches much of the band's 1990s output when Billie Joe as Jesus sings lines like, 'The world is spinning 'round and 'round/Out of control again/The 7-11 to the fear of breaking down/ So send my love a letterbomb and visit me in hell.' He's resigned to living life in a hellish city where he no longer fights battles for the betterment of those around him. He's back in 'barrio' – his neighborhood – and back in

Jingletown: a little wink to Green Day's recording studio and its Oakland neighborhood.

'Whatsername' (Lyrics: Armstrong; Music: Green Day)

All the melodrama, showmanship and theater fade away when 'Whatsername' comes chugging along to give us an update, sometime after the first dozen songs took place. As Billie Joe serves up one more impression of The Jesus of Suburbia, he laments how someone who meant so much to him previously, now feels anonymous. His chugging, lonely guitar eventually meets up with some cymbal-crashing Tré drumming and Dirnt's propelling bass notes. With one final loud and provocative chorus, the band find their cool chugging guitar groove before letting the last notes ring out into silence.

It's difficult to assess whether Jesus/St. Jimmy had a relationship with Whatsername, as some think they broke up and some think they never had one, to begin with. In the Broadway production, they dated. Either way, he's torn up about it, and feels like his life could've found a successful path with her by his side. It's a focused and loving lyric; a dream that just slipped out of his grasp, and floats away with the final sounds of the *American Idiot* album.

Related tracks

'Favorite Son' (Lyrics: Armstrong; Music: Green Day)

A purposely stiffer rhythm section is brought out of the cobwebs for this song, that features the widescreen *American Idiot* production that propelled their sound to the next level, though this song was freed from being tied down to the story. The precise stop/start guitar riff over the continuous rhythm section is an effective way of accompanying the average melody. There are no vocal breaks, with Armstrong working his way through the loud parts, the quieter melancholy moment, and the bridge.

One of Billie Joe's smartest profiles, 'Favorite Son,' dissects US President George W. Bush with an assortment of comical barbs meant to politically sting. The profiler indicates that Bush had a major advantage as the son of former President George H. W. Bush. It was released as a B-side to 'American Idiot' just before the album came out. Looking at the song titles together, 'American Idiot' and 'Favorite Son' present a more-direct political attack than the album itself.

'Too Much Too Soon' (Lyrics: Armstrong; Music: Green Day)

The crunchy 'Too Much Too Soon' brings the speed of the band's previous pop-punk world, rocking hard, but melodically. The chorus is a highlight, retaining a strong, warm melody despite the Dirnt and Cool's aggressive playing. Though the opening sounds just like that of 'Stuck With Me,' its hard edge is so cathartic that it proves that even on B-sides, Green Day were rocking better and harder than they had in quite some time. Armstrong comes up with an effective hopping chorus riff.

Verse one is in the third-person voice, with Billie Joe profiling a shopaholic who's overqualified at shopping and overheating a credit card. The chorus turns into accusations of materialism – sinking the woman's spirit.

'Shoplifter' (Lyrics: Armstrong; Music: Green Day)

This melody is taken from 'Brat,' the track using galloping bass and a mix of acoustic and electric guitar, sounding like a *Warning* leftover. The chorus happens to resemble 'Blood Sex And Booze.'

One of the band's most straightforward lyrics of the 2000s, 'Shoplifter' profiles a kleptomaniac, and Armstrong differentiates that he's not talking about someone who needs the money or goods but someone that does it maliciously to get it over on somebody.

'Governator' (Lyrics: Dirnt; Music: Green Day)

Mike Dirnt puts on a Billie Joe snarl for his lead vocal here. The track rocks hard like Clash songs, almost copying the stabbing guitar rhythm of 'Clash City Rockers,' placing it underneath another serviceable Mike melody. Armstrong joins in occasionally for some shouted harmony.

'Governator' is an attack on the then-Governor of California: actor Arnold Schwarzenegger. While Mike never sings Arnold's name, the mix of 'governor' and Arnold's famous *Terminator* quote 'I'll be back,' serves as the chorus. Though it wasn't part of *American Idiot*, it is part of the album's political aura and individualism theme.

Bullet in a Bible (Live) (2005)

Green Day issued their first live album on CD and DVD. It focused on the 2004/2005 *American Idiot* tour but didn't include the entire show. The band extend some songs, and there's plenty of audience interaction in the fiery live show.

'The Saints Are Coming' (Richard Jobson, Stuart Adamson)

Covering the 1979 Skids hit, Green Day teamed up with U2 for charitable reasons concerning Hurricane Katrina. It was a song about rescue and hope for the future, produced by Rick Rubin and Jacknife Lee. And no, Green Day forget about Jimmy and try to use their power to help the world, a bit like their *American Idiot* philosophy. The opening line 'There is a house in New Orleans they call the rising sun' is taken from the folk song and 1964 hit for The Animals: 'The House of the Rising Sun.' Billie Joe starts the vocal, and then alternates with Bono.

'Working Class Hero' (John Lennon)

Though this starts out respectful of John Lennon's original acoustic 1970 performance, this version branches out, growing wider and encompassing guitar layers, dramatic drum buildups and a thin line of keyboards. It bulks up like a weight lifter, pumping louder and louder until it blends into Lennon's original recording as Armstrong puts his vocal aside, allowing Lennon to sing the infamous final line, 'If you want to be a hero, well just follow me.' It's a thoughtful touch. It was recorded for the Amnesty International campaign to save Darfur. This – the album's lead single – was issued in April 2007, with the album following in June. The video opens with victims telling stories, interspersed with footage of Green Day performing in the studio. It's a black and white video, like that of 'Macy's Day Parade.'

'The Simpsons Theme' (Danny Elfman)

The TV cartoon *The Simpsons* has been on for so long that its theme is known to virtually everyone. Green Day had appeared in *The Simpsons* movie in 2007 (dying in a toxic river that eats the stage they perform on). They released this cover version as a promo single, but it didn't chart. Its 83 seconds is brief but enjoyable, with Billie Joe's vocalizing the melody over his guitar-playing.

21st Century Breakdown (2009)

Personnel:
Billie Joe Armstrong: lead vocals, guitar, piano
Mike Dirnt: bass, backing vocals; lead vocal ('Modern World')
Tré Cool: drums, percussion
Additional personnel:
Jason Freese: piano
Tom Kitt: string arrangements
Patrick Warren: conductor
Producers: Butch Vig, Green Day
Recorded at Studio 880, Oakland, CA; Ocean Way, Hollywood; Jel Studios, Newport Beach, CA; Costa Mesa Studios, Costa Mesa, CA
Label: Reprise
Release date: 15 May 2009
Charts: US: 1, UK: 1

After the massive success of the fantastic *American Idiot*, and all the touring and attention, it took five years for the band to come back with *21st Century Breakdown*. It's their keyboard album since Billie Joe wrote the songs on piano and several songs use keyboards. Though there are more soft moments on this album than any of their others, their rock grew larger and more fierce, retaining the last album's dynamics. Here they serve up some of the most exciting and adventurous music of their career. Armstrong's songwriting is excellent, as usual, and their overall sound had been given a fresh boost from producer Butch Vig. Rob Cavallo was gone as producer, but he'd be back.

The arrangements are complex, challenging, and, ultimately, highly rewarding. Billie Joe's lyrics are still as smart as almost any other rock lyricist. However, the album's one major flaw is its concept story arc – the story and characters are very similar to *American Idiot*, and this being their longest album so far, there was little new information. Christian and Gloria blend right into the characters The Jesus of Suburbia and Whatsername. Despite Billie Joe's request to use Christian and Gloria in the Broadway version of *American Idiot,* they chose to use some of the *21st Century Breakdown* songs but rejected the characters as they were essentially clones of the previous characters. Of all the topics in the world, why would the band do an entire album on the same stuff – like revolution, conformity, partying with drugs – that they'd just done? The storyline itself doesn't have much happening either, and it can get confusing at times. Armstrong spoke to *The Sun* about the album:

(It's) about the collateral damage with this past decade, but also the hope and optimism a lot of Americans have. It's a really strange time – exciting, because there's the first African-American President: a smart man who wants to do a good job; a man who's inheriting the biggest pile of shit this country has ever seen since the Depression. People are losing their jobs yet have a smile on their face, so this record is about that and the start of another era.

'Song Of The Century' (Lyrics: Armstrong; Music: Green Day)

The quiet and shy opening of a Green Day record arrives in the form of 'Song Of The Century,' with its filtered vocal as if discovered on a transistor radio. It's a one-minute-long number that sees our narrator struggling with the consequences the world has suffered as a result of George W. Bush's two terms as US president. It sets up the album's lyric foundation. The songs may not follow a perfect storyline, but they can all be linked to the *breakdown* seen in the US in the 2000s.

21st Century Breakdown' (Lyrics: Armstrong; Music: Green Day)

This amazing epic is a terrific launch towards a new world of Green Day's creation. The band think big, do big, and come up with gigantic musical moments, and the title track serves as the album's overture. It hops and jumps, bounding around due to the tremendous Tré, while Dirnt keeps things steady throughout Armstrong's hectic guitar leaps. The band zigzag between the differently-styled rooms of this five-minute mansion. It has room for their fast pop-punk, arena-sized chunks of straight mid-tempo hard rock, and those intimate, slow balladic moments. The fresh melody, successful arrangement and impassioned performance all add up to one of their best songs. The hard rock opening and softer second half are reminiscent of Queen's single, 'We Will Rock You'/'We Are the Champions'. The latter was a long-time member of Green Day's setlists and already issued as a live track from the various artists' benefit concert *Live 8* from a 2005 performance.

By 2009, Armstrong was more willing to be openly personal in his songwriting but maintained the façade of the characters Christian and Gloria as his mouthpieces. The title track comes from Billie Joe's life. He dives right into his birth during the Richard Nixon presidency, receiving government financial assistance, mentioning his father's union Teamsters group, growing up near an oil refinery and finally living as the youngest child of the Armstrong gang. But he was the fastest to take serious chances with his life and career. 'I was the last born and the first to run,' he says, perhaps sneakily referencing Bruce Springsteen's 1975 album *Born to Run*. That's just the first verse of this epic. The pre-chorus, 'My generation is zero/I never made it as a working-class hero' was a moment Billie Joe talked to AOL about: 'It's the time we live in right now. It's really hard for people to manage the situation they're in, let alone get out of it as far as either be working class, middle class or poor. There's a different crisis every week – natural disasters, corporate bailouts, people losing their homes and unemployment. That's sort of what the line represents to me.'

The smart chorus changes another famous expression, this time from the hymn 'Amazing Grace' – 'I once was lost but never was found' throws the

listener off since most use the line to explain their redemption. 'I think I'm
losing what's left of my mind' goes way back to Green Day's origins, where
Billie Joe thinks he's crazy on every other song. Part II begins with a line
about the class of '13: Billie Joe's son's class. He told *Rolling Stone*: "21st
Century Breakdown' was written at two different times, in two different parts.
Like there was that sort of *Irish drinking* part of the song – that was written
before, but it was just a riff that we were throwing around. And then that
could kind of introduce the whole record and how, like the whole record is
sort of about a 21st-century breakdown. It kind of sums up the last ten years.'

'Know You're Enemy' (Lyrics: Armstrong; Music: Green Day)
This punchy hit single pounces from the stereo with a menacing growl.
Tré destroys his cage with his lethally-powerful drumming, Dirnt's fingers
expertly crawl along his bass strings, and Armstrong contributes a gnawing,
gnarly guitar tone relying on a stop/start rhythm, eyeing meat before lunging.
The band know their enemy as naturally as an animal in nature, and their
aggressive and intense stance is strong, unrelentless and captivating.

'Know Your Enemy' is a clear message to attain knowledge to make life
decisions, question things and not accept information blindly. Know the
differing perspectives and 'revolt against the honor to obey.' It's more of the
message found all over *Warning* and *American Idiot*: be an individual. 'When
the blood's been sacrificed/Don't be blinded by the lies in your eyes,' he
sings, remembering all those who gave their lives in the Iraq War. Armstrong
even references the famous 1953 World War II film *From Here to Eternity* as
a way of saying violence has been present throughout history. Ultimately, the
enemy is silence and revolution is a friend.

'Viva La Gloria!' (Lyrics: Armstrong; Music: Green Day)
Though the title track had the line 'My name is no one,' Gloria is the first
character of this loose rock opera. Though we haven't yet learned of Christian
– the man embracing Gloria on the album cover – he's singing this song to
her. Billie Joe discussed it with *Blunt* magazine:

> The original name I was using for a while was Amélie. But the name Gloria,
> to me it sounded like the name version of Glory. It's a song kind of about
> me, but at the same time, if you add the name and you create a character,
> I think it gives blood and flesh to the record. So Gloria is just sort-of this
> person that's a torchbearer or someone that's trying to hold onto their beliefs
> or punk rock or whatever you want to call it. That's what I think the song is
> trying to convey, and it kind of adds to that first character. I think Gloria is
> the main character of the album.

With the beautiful lines, 'Eternal youth is the landscape of a lie/The cracks of
my skin can prove, as the years will testify,' the narrator Christian asks Gloria

why she's standing on the ledge talking of eternal youth as if she wants to die young by committing suicide. He commiserates by changing the line to 'We're standing on the edge,' as if he agrees life is miserable and that their opinions about the world are what drives him to be infatuated with her. More fascinating lyric highlights are 'You found a home in all your scars and ammunition/You made your bed in salad days amongst the ruin/Ashes to ashes of our youth,' meaning Gloria became comfortable as a rebel, and her best days were where she made her bed or sealed her fate.

'Viva La Gloria!' is a beautiful piano ballad in the first half and a blistering rocker for the remainder. As excellent as it is across the board, one may get a sinking feeling that this rock opera is starting to feel too similar to *American Idiot*. There's not much difference thus far between Gloria and Whatsername.

'Before The Lobotomy' (Lyrics: Armstrong; Music: Green Day)

It's as if Green Day bought a ticket for a time machine and travelled to the 1960s to create this elegant baroque-pop opening. But before you know it, the trio dive back into their crunchy anthemic sound, again using the stop/start rhythm to make room for Armstrong's bittersweet vocals. When he opens singing 'Dreaming, I was only dreaming,' it's right back to early Green Day and Billie Joe in his bedroom. But he's in character here. He sings sweetly and isn't shy about doing it. This band effort is smartly nuanced.

The character Christian appears to be a mix of The Jesus of Suburbia and St. Jimmy. He has the motivation of the former but the intent of the latter. Gloria remembers back to a fun, innocent childhood. Christian mentions he's not necessarily helping others, but he's aware of society's control. It affects Gloria's behaviour, so now she gets high because she's less capable of love. She's a mess now; she knows how rotten the world can get – hence the line, 'Life before the lobotomy/ Christian sang the eulogy, signed, 'My love'/A lost memory from the end of the century.' She hasn't felt love since the Millennium. Billie Joe mentioned some of the fire references to *MTV*: '(Gloria is) the person who's trying to hold onto her beliefs. Christian's a nihilist. He wants to burn everything down. Fire gets brought up a lot on the record. And in one respect, it can be very purifying, and the other, it can be reckless and damaging. And I think that's what they represent on the record.'

'Christian's Inferno' (Lyrics: Armstrong; Music: Green Day)

Here the band sound positively alive, and burn it up on another song that's in place to balance the piano-ballad moments. Boy is it effective in waking up anybody that lost focus listening. It's the album's St. Jimmy moment. The blistering battle-driven rhythm is a raucous blend of hard, charging guitar, crisp bass and destructive drums.

'There's fire in my veins' and 'I am the atom bomb' link fiery and violent images to Christian's inner feelings about what he can do to improve his life and society. 'Christian's Inferno' is also the 'Holiday' of *21st Century*

Breakdown. It's the coming-out party, with the hero – the Jesus of Suburbia/
Christian – announcing to the world that he's ready. Christian desires to *harm*
more than help. Billie Joe told *Q* magazine:

> It's about how self-destructive behavior can overshadow parts of your
> ambition. A lot of people have a self-destruct button. I think, for a lot of rock
> musicians, when you're celebrating, it turns into partying, and then suddenly
> you're fucking yourself up and you're destroying something you worked so
> hard to build up. There's this shiny red button that you just want to push.

'Last Night On Earth' (Lyrics: Armstrong; Music: Green Day)
This simple love song finds the band fully committing to a beautiful ballad.
Piano is the prominent instrument, swaying with class. It's a methodical pop
song, with a superb melody giving a rare glimpse of the group's romantic
side, but with a touch of apocalypse.

There are no jump-up-and-headbang moments. It's about Christian's love for
Gloria. 'If I lose everything in the fire/I'm sending all my love to you,' he sings
sweetly, again referencing his burning desires. Armstrong told *Blue Railroad*:
''Last Night On Earth' is a love song I wrote for my wife. I wrote it on piano and
then sang it. And you say, 'Wow, I never sang falsetto before – that's pretty cool'.'

'East Jesus Nowhere' (Lyrics: Armstrong; Music: Green Day)
After a radio DJ briefly displays some disappointment in society for through
static, the band roll out this loud, boisterous, brash up-tempo rocker with a
big Tré rhythm and a diverse array of backing-vocal styles. It's colossal, like
the band's ambition. The guitars scratch and grind, then play melodically. The
rhythm transforms into a military rhythm straight out of 'Holiday,' pushing
and shoving it around like a bully.

The unfaithful 'East Jesus Nowhere' (a title inspired by the 2007 film *Juno*)
deals with the downside of religion. Armstrong plays a preacher who's calling
people to church. 'A fire burns today of blasphemy and genocide,' he declares
in a way similar to how Christian and Gloria think of the world. But the
preacher has a different answer: religion. Armstrong told *Kerrang!* magazine
that he and his wife passed a church called The Church of Divine Hope: 'I
was looking at it deliriously, and I thought, 'Oh my God, that's like calling it
the 'church of wishful thinking.' We started laughing hysterically, so I wrote it
down and it ended up being in 'East Jesus Nowhere.' Armstrong is the preacher
during the chorus and first verse. Verse two – where he plays a converted
attendant – includes the line, 'I threw my crutches in the river of the shadow
of doubt,' mocking the impossible miracles that certain evangelists were
advertising. He told *NME*:

> This song is a call-out against the hypocrisy of religion. Whether you're using
> it as a vendetta or you're using it for monetary gain or whatever, people

tend to abuse their faith in order to fulfill their God complex. The song is about revenge; sort-of having this vendetta. Part two is sort-of about gun control. But it's really kind of sexually driven. It's the first time we're really bringing in musically a Middle Eastern influence; some kind of gypsy flavor to it. It could it be played by a Mariachi band or an Italian funeral band or something like that.

'Peacemaker' (Lyrics: Armstrong; Music: Green Day)

The Spanish-sounding, turbocharged 'Peacemaker' uses a recycled melody that mostly works. Perhaps it's the weaker friend of The Clash's 'Spanish Bombs.' Armstrong and company are great when they sing their fast harmonies to keep up with the frantic acoustic guitar. The strings provide a dramatic rush. 'Peacemaker' could outrun a cheetah, but it doesn't have an aggressive sound to match its cruel lyric.

'Well I've got a fever/A non-believer in a state of grace,' Christian sings, unconvinced by the preacher from 'East Jesus Nowhere'. In fact, he's going to get violent when he returns to the church, threatening to ruin it by killing the preacher, who wants money. Christian calls himself 'A killjoy from Detroit,' a bit like St. Jimmy gave himself a nickname. Christian also likens himself to Julius Caesar the famous general. Dark images abound in this colorfully-stellar lyric, including Gaza: a place in the Middle East which saw violence against Christians. Assassins, banshees, a Peacemaker gun, Molotov cocktails, undertakers and a neo-St. Valentine's massacre, all make appearances.

'Last Of The American Girls' (Lyrics: Armstrong; Music: Green Day)

This hard rock track has a steady, bright tempo, as they carve an A-grade melody into rocking, ringing guitars and a jolly rhythm section. It's a sonic celebration profile of a particular female standout. The rebellious track talks of how women were previously more inclined to cause a ruckus or stand up for themselves. Billie Joe told *Q*: 'I started writing it for my wife, but there's elements of Hurricane Katrina and Critical Mass. It adds those elements to one character who has this left-wing strength.'

After *American Idiot*, in 2005, Hurricane Katrina severely damaged the city of New Orleans, and President Bush was thought to have taken too long to respond. The city was devastated, thousands of lives were ruined and many lives were lost. Critical Mass references nuclear material. Gloria doesn't trust the government, and she fights for citizen's rights. She plays old records, like the famously-banned 1965 political song 'Eve Of Destruction.' There may be another reference to Bikini Kill singer Kathleen Hanna in the first line, 'She puts her makeup on like graffiti on the walls of the heartland.' Hanna was known to write messages on her body, like revolution graffiti.

'Murder City' (Lyrics: Armstrong; Music: Green Day)

'Murder City' is another awesome display of power and precision. The band stay accurate with their timing at such speeds and volume, and then slow or stop simultaneously. It's clear they'd been together for two decades. The 'I feel so helpless' chorus is how Billie Joe felt in reality, but his protagonist Gloria is the filter. 'We've come so far, we've been so wasted/Christian's crying in the bathroom and I just want a cigarette,' she cries at a turning point in the story arc. Constant mentions of midnight act as warning signs that time is up for this duo. Unfortunately, the song was based on Armstrong and Dirnt witnessing a kid being shot while in handcuffs. Armstrong told *Blue Railroad*:

This was the last song written for the record. Me and Mike and Tre were in downtown Oakland, and we went out to have drinks. It was right after these demonstrations happened. This kid was shot by a cop – while handcuffed. We were walking in; I'm wide awake after the riot. We weren't there for the riot, but it was right after. That song gets stuck in my head more than the other songs do.

'¿Viva La Gloria? (Little Girl)' (Lyrics: Armstrong; Music: Green Day)

Like its twin sister, '¿Viva La Gloria?', this song starts calmly, only to be overcome and discomforted by the quiet. They both instantly energize and *up* the volume as the song progresses.

The album started with Gloria troubled but confident. But due to Christian's bad influence, she's fallen heavily into drugs, so she's a 'stray from the Salvation Army.' There are some harrowing images of her face in the gutter, and mentions of blood. Christian accuses her of being a liar, unholy and a charlatan. Though Christian and St. Jimmy have similar characters, they differ in this instance, since The Jesus of Suburbia always loved Whatsername even after she sent him the *letterbomb* that ended their time together. Here Christian is turning on Gloria. Billie Joe told *Q* in 2009: '¿Viva La Gloria?' is about a person who has a vision, but this is a person who's distorting that vision with drugs and self-destruction.'

'Restless Heart Syndrome' (Lyrics: Armstrong; Music: Green Day)

Piano and strings lead the way until the acoustic guitars and drums come around in this baroque pop song. Feeling restless, the band travel to their sensitive side while Billie Joe looks for 'a place to hide.' The narrator singing in hushed tones, matches the music's low profile. But he can only hold it in for so long, before the electric guitar blasts out, unable to contain its emotion. The band donate a proficient, pounding rhythm that could crush any living thing in its path. The contrast between the soft-boiled first half and the hard-shelled second half is the heart of the arrangement.

'Horseshoes and Hand Grenades' (Lyrics: Armstrong; Music: Green Day)

The band grind out another massive stadium hard rocker, and their brutal, disorienting assault is monstrous. Billie Joe rips through his street-savvy guitar licks. The refrain, 'Demolition, self-destruction/Wanna annihilate this age-old contradiction,' sums up the lyric. Christian has an undying fire inside. In the 2010s, a Wisconsin band adopted this song title as their band name.

'The Static Age' (Lyrics: Armstrong; Music: Green Day)

This catchy song sounds like 'Church On Sunday' when it hits the chorus. That song had a great hook, and here it's recycled to this song's advantage. 'The Static Age' still has its own flavor, sharing the priceless anthemic bomb blast of the production. Yes, there's some bombast too, but that's the point – the stadium-sized songs are supposed to be universal and ambitious in nature. Billie Joe uses 'static' as a double entendre, implying radio static and the static nature of positive societal change. 'Slogans on the brink of destruction' harkens back to 'Warning' and how politicians use empty slogans to get votes – we are individuals, but society generalizes, so individualism is lost in mass messaging.

'21 Guns' (Lyrics: Armstrong; Music: Green Day)

One of the band's most-famous stop/start rhythms, '21 Guns' has a sensational, sweet melody and sweet folk-rock verses, but they tangle with a primitive and fiercely-visceral riff-led chorus. It's too bad the stellar chorus borrows heavily from Electric Light Orchestra's 'Telephone Line': served in a hard-rock disguise. It also includes a lyric which references the title of the 1973 Paul McCartney and Wings' hit, 'Live and Let Die'. It holds the song back from being one of Green Day's very best, but it's still an excellent album highlight. A second version of '21 Guns' has the band joined by the *American Idiot* Broadway cast. Billie Joe told *Q*:

> '21 Guns' is definitely one of the songs where you feel like you're playing in front of a lot of people. It's one of the things I wrote on piano, and it ended up being just sort of this moment alone, you know. I think a lot of people think that song is about world peace or something. But I think also there's like maybe sort of surrendering to the static to try to find some kind of inner peace, or, you know, finding strength in silence. You know, surrendering doesn't always have to mean that you're giving up. But maybe it means you're just trying to find a little humanity.

'American Eulogy (A. Mass Hysteria/B. Hysterical World)' (Lyrics: Armstrong; Music: Green Day)

You might think the big finale and penultimate track would be arranged to match that of *American Idiot*'s 'Homecoming'. But it's still another quality song and performance. The one weakness is its intimacy with the melody from 'Westbound Sign.' It speeds along with quirky new-wave guitar arches hovering over the sizzling rhythm. With a group chant for a chorus, and stadium-sized production, it serves as a great knockout punch that leaves the listener left to recover on the less-intense conclusion. Billie Joe told *Q*: 'It swirls all the information that's going on in the record, around in an emotional blender. At the end, it's going to sound like a wall of TV screens. It's sensory overload.' Mike added, 'Starting off with 'Mass Hysteria,' that song is just kind of an outcry for, you know, TMI: too much information, and living in fear of everything around you and everything that you're being told you should be afraid of. You know – find value in things that aren't so flash in the pan or aren't controlled by technology.'

'See The Light' (Lyrics: Armstrong; Music: Green Day)
This melodic and dynamic song brings a little softness, before laying down one final muscular album moment. More than most songs here, 'See the Light' reveals Green Day's power-pop side – a subgenre that's littered throughout much of their work. One might feel a Coldplay sound on the closer, just like on the title track. The opening piano notes of '21st Century Breakdown' are recycled here to wrap the album up in a bow. Billie Joe told *Q*: 'I think 'See The Light' kind of sums up the journey. It talks about streets and it talks about deserts and it talks about rivers and it talks about natural disasters, and every crisis from the Swine Flu to Hurricane Katrina and everything in between, which is a lot. So I think it's just trying to find more meaning in life and more belief in yourself.'

Non-LP B-sides
'Lights Out' (Lyrics: Armstrong; Music: Green Day)
Using that *American Idiot* vocal filter to open the song, Billie Joe and company rock out in reverb with one of their best B-sides. It's a berserk attack that's held together by a strong melody. Once the filter's off, Armstrong sounds surprisingly hoarse yet comes through with a noble vocal performance. But it's Tré and Mike that really shine on this fine number. Mike's bass is prominent, and Tré plays it straight but powerful enough to shatter all the light bulbs in town. Armstrong churns out a straight lyric about being cautious at night. Though well-written and simple, it's so general that there's not enough detail for any of it to matter, and there's a tossed-off line about suicide. He mentions he's between heaven and hell.

'Hearts Collide' (Lyrics: Armstrong; Music: Green Day)
The romantic 'Hearts Collide' is a speedy rock tune with a poppy melody and vocal harmonies throughout. It's a rare time that Billie Joe and Mike sing co-lead vocals. The sweetness matches the impact love can have. It's passionate punk rock with a heart. The grungy 1950s-sounding guitar solo is slightly

ugly compared to the happier, prettier feel they employ. While the song is a wonderful expression of love, there's not much else to this mostly generic piece, and the title is repeated a few too many times; its weak hook failing to pierce. It could be transplanted into the *21st Century Breakdown* album if Christian were singing it to Gloria.

'A Quick One, While He's Away' (Pete Townshend)

The inspiration behind *American Idiot*, The Who's 'A Quick One (While He's Away)' was one of the first suites in rock. Released in 1966, The Who's original was a story with different characters that was eventually overshadowed by *Tommy*, but it was a fascinating quilt of songs. Green Day were still infatuated with it enough to perform it live on their 2000s tours, and to record it. They released their cover as an iTunes bonus track as part of the *21st Century Breakdown* promotion. They add some muscle to the colorful story, about a girl who wonders when her boyfriend will come back only to have an ugly incident with an engine driver. Her boyfriend comes back and forgives her for her sexual transgression.

'Another State Of Mind' (Mike Ness)

This cover of Social Distortion's 1983 song 'Another State of Mind' is about life on the road.

'That's All Right' (Arthur Crudup)

Made famous by Elvis Presley in 1954, 'That's All Right' was one of rock's earliest legendary hits. Billie Joe is made to sound like he's coming from a gramophone. It sounds like Dirnt got hold of a standup bass for more 1950s authenticity. Tré and Mike have rarely seen time on the bench, but the band's drummer takes a seat on the sidelines for this two-minute cover.

'Like A Rolling Stone' (Bob Dylan)

Dylan's biggest chart hit is another legendary song. Dylan influenced *Warning*, and in turn, *American Idiot*. 'Welcome To Paradise' was the 1990s alternative rock version of 'Like A Rolling Stone,' since both protagonists leave their parents and go off into the world for the first time only to find it was tougher than they expected. It's six minutes of clean, bright-sounding rock, losing a lot of the distortion that usually makes up the meat of much Green Day material.

American Idiot: The Original Broadway Cast Recording (2010)

Green Day were one of the world's biggest bands, and now they were making it big on Broadway as well. The stage production is based on *American Idiot* and *21st Century Breakdown*. They used the former's storyline and characters and fleshed it out with the further characters Johnny, Will, Tunny, St. Jimmy/Jimmy (Johnny's alter ego was played by another actor), Heather (a pregnant girlfriend), Extraordinary Girl (who was Whatsername on the album), the 'representative of Jingletown' (inspired by Billie Joe's spoken section on 'Too Much Too Soon'), and the Favorite Son (based on the *American Idiot* B-side of the same name). B-sides *21st Century Breakdown* songs are successfully and seamlessly woven into the show.

The initial run lasted from April 2010 to April 2011, with additional runs throughout the decade in various places inside and outside the US. Various cast members take the vocals, usually joined by backing vocals from other performers or dancers. Sometimes they go with full group vocals. It all ends with a performance of 'Good Riddance (Time Of Your Life).'

There's a street aesthetic to the scenery and costume design, trying hard not to feel like a big Broadway production, bringing it in line with the original album's philosophy. It's always hard for Green Day fans to hear others sing the band's songs, but the cast does a solid job of capturing the emotion throughout. The show is still active around the world in various places.

'When It's Time' (Lyrics: Armstrong; Music: Green Day)

Also included in the musical, a version by Green Day closed the cast album. This is an old song written a decade earlier for Billie Joe's wife Adrienne. It's the sweetest love song Armstrong wrote in the 1990s. It displays none of the band's usual go-to tendencies of aggression, power and dizzying speed. They keep the piano at the forefront, like on some of *21st Century Breakdown,* and Armstrong proves he constantly has plenty of effective and satisfying melodies flying from his mind. He sings somewhat sweeter than he normally does but is as nasally as ever, and the production brings it all together. It's pop/rock at its best. The guitar brightens and careens off the rhythm of the break. There are some gorgeous, romantic lines, like, 'My time ticks around you' and 'They'll never have someone like you to guard them and help along the way.'

¡Uno! (2012)

Personnel:
Billie Joe Armstrong: lead vocals, guitar
Mike Dirnt: bass, backing vocals
Tré Cool: drums
Jason White: guitar, backing vocals
Additional personnel:
Rob Cavallo: keyboards
Producers: Rob Cavallo, Green Day
Recorded at Jingletown Recording, Oakland, California
Label: Reprise
Release date: 21 September 2012
Charts: US: 2, UK: 2
Singles: 'Oh Love, ' 'Kill The DJ,' 'Let Yourself Go'

After the hoopla of having *American Idiot* as a Broadway show as the
decade turned, the band's first album of the 2010s finds them going back to
their roots, but unlike their first five albums, they use other musical styles,
like garage rock. Armstrong has help on rhythm guitar from new member
Jason White: their touring guitarist since the beginning of the century. They
hadn't had four members in Green Day since 1988. But they could've used
Jason more effectively, as their guitar parts usually match closely, rarely
branching away from each other. Billie Joe takes the chance to play some
guitar solos – usually skillful ones – but rhythmically, it doesn't sound too
different to their past material. Here, Mike and Tré are treading water. Mike
rarely gets solo bass moments, though he sings a lot more harmonies.

Armstrong has never previously had a dip in his songwriting. He gets
better with each album. *¡Uno!* is his first step back. He can't quite reach
those highs he's found countless times before. It's evident in the resulting
album, poor singles sales and mediocre critical reaction. Even though 'Oh
Love' hit number one, as a worthy Green Day lead single, some fans and
critics were disappointed with the rest of the record. The single and trilogy
as a whole are occasionally generic, losing much of the band's character.

Supposedly, Billie Joe recorded all three albums worth of vocals in
a few days. It's easy to tell that on some songs, as he's just rattling-off
information like he's reading the traffic news. The lack of emotion and
sincerity is highly surprising for a singer who has plenty of emotional
layers to his lyrics. He referred to The Clash's triple album *Sandinista!*
when he talked to NPR: 'Next thing we knew, we ended up with something
like 30 songs. 'Are we doing *Sandinista!* here?' So we said, 'Let's do three
discs and release one record at a time, and wouldn't it be funny if we
called it *Uno, Dos* and *Tré?*' But in hindsight, he changed his stance, telling
Rolling Stone in 2016: 'I always wanted *¡Uno!*, *¡Dos!* and *¡Tre!* to be our
power-pop *Exile on Main Street,* and I understand it sounds a bit stiff and

the production isn't great. I love those songs, but a lot of it feels half-baked. It was a weird time.'

'Nuclear Family' (Lyrics: Armstrong; Music: Green Day)
The trilogy opens admirably with this nihilistic mid-tempo rocker. They use their tried-and-true stop/start technique, but each time they fill the pockets with a different instrument. Armstrong performing one of his best vocals. He plays with his emotional tones, going from tongue-in-cheek to authentic, from taunting to sympathetic, as he addresses the fate of this nuclear family. Dirnt creates one of his best bass lines, decorating with excellent melodicism that became a significant part of the song's shape. It's an explosive opening, and gets the listener's hopes up that there will be more adventures like this.

The trilogy unlocks with an early message to party and take a break from all the world's heavy issues. It's like the decay of society found on *American Idiot* and *21st Century Breakdown*. With a title recalling the Cold War, 'Nuclear Family' turns its back on hard times and looks at ways to make life more enjoyable. Armstrong is breaking free from his family restraints, and like a nuclear bomb, he'll 'detonate' once he leaps into the party life. It results in a figurative *death* of the nuclear family in the song, as the narrator 'rides the world like a merry-go-round' before life ends. Armstrong plays on this by adding that the 'nuclear family is looking up at you,' changing to second-person while indicating the family are buried alive, looking up at us from their graves. He counts down to zero to conclude the song.

'Stay The Night' (Lyrics: Armstrong; Music: Green Day)
This highly addictive song continues the commendable quality and is hook-laden, with radio potential. There's a mix of heroic, chiming and driving guitars, some of Tré's best drumming – controlled yet entertaining – and Mike's busy bass: all to the song's advantage.

The song comes second on *¡Uno!*, to continue living it up 'cause we're running out of time' before the world is destroyed. It's about a guy who wants to get the girl he always wanted. Neither are dating anyone, so why not find out if she was really the girl for him all along.

'Carpe Diem' (Lyrics: Armstrong; Music: Green Day, Jeff Shadbolt)
The clock winds down to oblivion. 'Carpe Diem' borrows the chorus melody of 'I Fought The Law' – a number they covered a decade earlier – using a sound straight out of The Clash's 1978 album *Give 'Em Enough Rope*. Armstrong and White converse well on guitar with a typical chopping rhythmic verse pattern.

Still in a party vein, Billy Joe wants to seize the day before it's gone forever – 'Nothing left to lose/Detonate the fuse/Another breaking news blowout' and 'Life's a gas,' explaining how annihilation threats resulted in these narrators breaking free of inhibition. The clever lyric continues with the refrain, 'Carpe diem battle cry/Are we all too young to die?' It's a major clue to realizing that this isn't just a party, but a final party.

'Let Yourself Go' (Lyrics: Armstrong; Music: Green Day)
This top-25 single is a straight-up barnburner. Its music insists on its message – frantic and gutsy – with the band's full energy invested. Dirnt provides a catchy riff that sprints alongside the speedy vocal melody.

Let yourself go, *Let loose* and *Live it up* seem to be the album's mottos so far. The target of Billie Joe's venom and advice is one of the band's typical enemies: a person who complains a lot and doesn't enjoy life. 'I'm sick to death of your every last breath,' he remarks to his hypochondriac target. But the band move past politics for the rest of the trilogy (with a couple of exceptions), listening to their own advice to just let go.

'Kill The DJ' (Lyrics: Armstrong; Music: Green Day, Chrissie Hynde, Mirwais Ahmadzai)
Another song that owes a debt to The Clash circa 1980, the infamous failed single 'Kill The DJ' has a half-reggae/half-funk rhythm. Armstrong speaks the chorus, and the playfully-ridiculous lyrics aren't humorous. Neither the rhythm nor the riffs are catchy, though there's a nifty experimental guitar break.

The band are at a party where a DJ plays 'Kill The DJ.' Among the pills and beer goggles at this party is the 'blood left on the dance floor.' Armstrong told *Rolling Stone* in 2012:

It's a song about being drunk, going through this chaos, feeling fucked up, and all you want to do is get more drunk. Mike wanted me to write something four-on-the-floor – 'Something like Gang of Four or Blondie's 'Heart Of Glass' – almost a disco kind of song. I didn't really have any references for that kind of thing outside of maybe The Clash. So I wrote that song, and I just like the irony of writing a dance song that's saying 'Kill The DJ.'

'Fell For You' (Lyrics: Armstrong: Music: Green Day)
This fast, romantic alternative pop/rocker could sneak onto an early Tom Petty album and no one would notice. The joyous melody adds a British Invasion appeal. Dirnt's bass syncs with Armstrong's vocal line and Tré plays it straight, but it's generic Green Day.

It's been a long time since we visited Billie Joe's bedroom, but here we go again. Infatuation touches him just when he thought it would end. The clunky lyric smooches with their early romance songs. Billie Joe detailed the song for *Rolling Stone*: 'When I revisit it (the trilogy), 'Fell For You' is what stands out. I was listening to a lot of power-pop music. I always say that power pop is the greatest music on Earth that no one likes, whether it's something like Cheap Trick or (another band). That was like, let's just write a gooey bubblegum song about dreams and love and crushes and all the stuff that kind of keeps us alive.'

'Loss Of Control' (Lyrics: Armstrong; Music: Green Day, Chrissie Hynde, James Honeyman-Scott)

The punk of 'Loss Of Control' mixes with some post-punk guitar work, but it lacks the creativity of post-punk, just piledriving through nonstop until it concludes. The standard arrangement takes away from the song's power. But Billie Joe works-in some great lead guitar accents, his solo is one of his best and most raucous, and Mike adds plenty of close vocal harmonies. The band is in attack mode at a high school reunion, with Billie Joe thinking everyone lies about having massive success.

'Troublemaker' (Lyrics: Armstrong; Music: Green Day)

'Troublemaker' continues the band's apathy towards dynamics, as it focuses more on texture. Choppy, jumpy Armstrong and White guitars are synced with Dirnt's bass part. But the song needs help in the melody and hook department, and gets none from the arrangement either. It goes for a dance vibe, using extra percussion like they were to later use for the majority of their 2020 album *Father of All Motherf**kers*. It's the rival of their song 'Peacemaker'. Billie Joe's proverb-twist 'Til death do we party' is the best descriptor.

'Angel Blue' (Lyrics: Armstrong; Music: Green Day)

While Tré and Mike put in fine performances on this speedy pop-punk track, Billie Joe sounds like he's on autopilot, putting no emotion into the vocal. We can't tell if he's upset, happy, or likes or dislikes Angel Blue. Tré plays softer, and Armstrong's guitar goes for The Clash's 'Tommy Gun' sound successfully, offsetting the happy music's poppy nature. Mike pushes the chorus hook with his vocal harmony.

Billie Joe claims he's in purgatory – like he did on 'Lights Out' – and sings about his 'better angels'. But unfortunately, this lyric has some dud lines, needless melodrama, and a confusing change of narrative voice halfway through.

'Sweet 16' (Lyrics: Armstrong; Music: Green Day)

The power-pop 'Sweet 16' is a quick biographical sketch of Billie Joe's life with Adrienne. Their 20-year marriage deserved more lyrics. It has a fittingly-joyful melody, but there's no hook, and there's nothing of note in this no-frills effort. It lacks energy and nuance, but has a tremendous vocal. He also presents the loving gift of a nifty guitar solo. Though Adrienne is older than Billie Joe and was past 20 when they met, he reminds us of Chuck Berry's 'Sweet Little Sixteen' and that romantic notion of teens in love. 'The kids are alright, alright as they'll ever be' is a nod to The Who's song 'The Kids Are Alright,' but there's another needless line in 'Stab out my heart like a dartboard' – the third time Billie Joe finds himself stabbed in the heart on *¡Uno!*. Green Day would later name a song 'Stab You In The Heart.'

'Rusty James' (Lyrics: Armstrong; Music: Green Day)

Sounding melodically like the sequel to the *Nimrod* track 'Scattered,' 'Rusty James' isn't as effective, though it is catchy. Mike's bass-playing and the coda have a Who influence, while the rest harkens back to The Clash circa 1978.

The album's second-named character is 'Rusty James': the name is taken from a street thug in the gang movie *Rumble Fish*. The song is about an old-school punk rocker who doesn't like the new punk scene. It's as if Green Day were inhabiting the Gilman crowd's no-sellout state of mind. On the chorus, they remind people that they're 'the last gang in town.'

'Oh Love' (Lyrics: Armstrong; Music: Green Day)

This arena-sized power ballad and number one single has some of the trilogy's catchiest hooks but some cliché lyrics. Scratchy verse rhythm guitar and Mike's fruitfully-melodic bass work are highlights. The chopped rhythmic segues between verse and chorus show the band's teamwork.

'Oh love, won't you rain on me tonight' begins the most successful song of the trilogy. 'Oh Love' is also linked to 'Stop When The Red Lights Flash' as a little preview of *¡Dos!,* indicating that Billie Joe wants to live it up and enjoy life before it passes him by, just like on half the *¡Uno!* songs. He cutely sings that his heart is on a noose, so he's putting it on the loose. 'Oh losers and choosers/Won't you please hold on to my life' are clever lines referencing abortion, but really this love song is pretty standard – the narrator loves a woman. Billie Joe told MTV: 'Oh Love' is kind of like leading with your heart, and not necessarily with your brain as much.

¡Dos! (2012)

Personnel:
Billie Joe Armstrong: lead vocals, guitar
Mike Dirnt: bass, backing vocals
Tré Cool: drums, percussion
Jason White: guitar
Lady Cobra: vocals ('Nightlife')
Producers: Rob Cavallo, Green Day
Recorded at Jingletown Recording, Oakland, California
Label: Reprise
Release date: 9 November 2012
Charts: US: 9, UK: 10
Singles: 'Stray Heart'

The second album in the trilogy takes a few chances, with the band trying out some new sounds, having their first guest artist since U2 (on 'The Saints Are Coming') and trying to capture a garage-rock party vibe. Some chances pay off, like the raw garage rock found on 'Makeout Party,' 'Lady Cobra' and the mod Who/Yardbirds stylings of 'Wow! That's Loud.' The hip hop 'Night Life' and garage/glam of 'F*** Time' are less successful.

Billie Joe's lyric writing has dipped and taken a big hit overall, and it's maybe his least-convincing effort to date. Unfortunately, his vocal lacks its usual rich emotion. So many of his efforts here ring hollow, partially because the melodies are substandard, and he doesn't seem inspired. On 'Night Life' he sounds like a filtered zombie; on 'Wild One', he drags like his drink has been drugged, and on 'Stray Heart' he can't decide on an emotional direction. Jason White's playing isn't prominent, with the guitar parts locking much of the time, but the guitars do change tone (unlike on *¡Uno!* and *Tré!*). *¡Uno!* has the better songwriting, and *¡Dos!* has the better performances.

'See You Tonight' (Lyrics: Armstrong; Music: Green Day)

This album takes the rare route of starting with a soft track. It's a soothing, hopeful, pretty ballad before things get hectic, but from early on, the vocal generally feels empty. The song is a brief reminder to the woman of 'Oh Love' that Billie Joe is still anticipating a date. The band explained numerous times that *¡Dos!* is the party record, and this song takes place as they get themselves ready.

'F*** Time' (Lyrics: Armstrong; Music: Green Day)

This wicked but mediocre track mixes garage rock, a snotty sexually-overdriven Armstrong vocal and a mix of glam rock and power pop. The band swipe guitar riffs from Berry Gordy and Janie Branford's song for Barrett Strong, 'Money (That's What I Want)' (also covered by The Beatles). The guitar solo is the highlight on this mediocre track, as the attitude is prioritized over melody and riffs. Billie Joe told *Rolling Stone*: 'A guy in the cast (Broadway cast for *American Idiot*) – Theo Stockman – started calling himself the King of Fuck. Then it got into a thing where every time they got ready for a show, the cast members got in a circle, put their hands in the middle, and went, 'One, two, three, It's fuck time!' I just wrote the song.'

'Stop When The Red Lights Flash' (Lyrics: Armstrong; Music: Green Day)
This track ups the quality with a better melody, but it doesn't capture lightning in a bottle. But it did alright on the charts; the chorus harmonies are solid. Dirnt plays some meaty bass.

This is one of the band's most bare lyrics. It's almost impossible to decipher why Billie Joe warns to stay back and stop at the red light. The only line that gives a little information is 'I'll trade you blood for dirty cash,' like the narrator is a hitman. The song needed more information and a better chorus if it was to chart as high as their earlier singles.

'Lazy Bones' (Lyrics: Armstrong; Music: Green Day)
Sounding like a mix of chopped post-punk guitar and garage rock, 'Lazy Bones' has some new textures working in the verses. The melody is much closer to Billie Joe quality, and the singsong-style chorus was missed on the last two numbers. Billie Joe finally gets back to wordplay with a lyric about being too tired to do or be anything else. The protagonist is 'too tired to be bored' and 'too mental to go crazy,' and he sounds like it. As we hit the chorus, the self-reflection turns to the second-person, addressing someone Billie Joe dislikes, saying it's too late to rectify the situation.

'Wild One' (Lyrics: Armstrong; Music: Green Day)
The plodding but solid 'Wild One' has some glorious lead guitar, an emotive vocal, and notable Mike falsetto harmonies working off a big melody. Tré continues to play more controlled on *¡Dos!* The creative juices are flowing better than on the first four songs. Billie Joe has a wild fan attracted to him. She has manic eyes, gave up on Jesus, and is living on Venus because she's a love goddess with unusual behavior. She's covered in angels, halos and demons, and she's 'strung-out on razors' – meaning she either cuts herself as a self-hate tactic or she uses razors to line up her cocaine. That line was built around David Bowie singing about his wild one 'Jean Genie' in 1972, when he sang 'Strung out lasers and slash back blazers/And ate all the razors while pulling the waiters.'

'Makeout Party' (Lyrics: Armstrong; Music: Green Day)
There are lots of instruments mingling and drums crashing like glasses smashing here. It's a busy arrangement for the chaotic aural scene. It's

great raw-sounding garage rock with a stellar descending guitar figure and precision bass and drums.

The song is about a guy who plays spin the bottle to get a random woman to kiss him. The games Chicken and Truth or Dare are also mentioned. The song gives the album character, though it's not nearly its best-written one. If the band had this raw garage sound more frequently, it wouldn't feel like Rob Cavallo was smoothing out the edges on ¡Uno! or ¡Dos!.

'Stray Heart' (Lyrics: Armstrong; Music: Green Day)

This track pushes the tempo, pushes Billie Joe's luck with a woman he needs to apologize to, and pushes chopped rhythm-guitar lines. It's not necessarily aggressive, but everybody's playing better than on the earlier tracks – Mike and Tré are so locked-in perfecting the fantastic rhythm over the sparse arrangement. The instrumental break is the album's most exhilarating moment. Billie Joe lets loose on lead guitar. Mike and Tré totally change up the rhythm, adding the dynamics that have been lacking so far on the trilogy.

The song was written about cheating on a girlfriend. He's asking for forgiveness, but she's not ready to take him back because of his stray heart. The direct lyric says the flirtation or affair was a mistake, and he will never do it again.

'Ashley' (Lyrics: Armstrong; Music: Green Day)

The vocal starts immediately and the band blast through the song. It seems like a mix of the same chords and notes Billie Joe has used countless times, but he provides a rewarding solo. There is a hook, but if it was on a tow truck, it would be too weak to lift a car. The band are solid but lack that certain something they had on 'Stray Heart.'

A shoulder can be very supportive, and in the chorus, that body part is in one of the album's cleverest lines – 'Are you crying on my cold shoulder?' basically says it all. Billie Joe has no empathy for a sad woman who hurt him in the past. She teased him too much in the past, and now his lack of help is his revenge.

'Baby Eyes' (Lyrics: Armstrong; Music: Green Day)

'Baby Eyes' lacks enthusiasm, but the guitars curling into the verses, and Dirnt's commendable harmonies, are highlights.

Baby Eyes is the nickname Billie Joe gives the next woman he encounters, and he introduces himself with the autobiographical 'Year of the Rat/Last of the litter.' After claiming his middle name is 'Danger,' it's obvious this might be the hitman from 'Stop When The Red Lights Flash.' Billie Joe gave his second child the middle name 'Danger'. The obtuse lyric also weakens this forgettable song. We'll assume he's another wild character at this crazy ¡Dos! party.

'Lady Cobra' (Lyrics: Armstrong; Music: Green Day)

Lady Cobra – a rapper from the short-lived Crockett, CA group Mystic Knights of the Cobra – is a guest on this track. Armstrong's tribute to her has some of the trilogy's most convincingly-raw garage rock. Like with 'Makeout Party,' the intensity cooks up the average composition with a furious, exciting rhythm. Billie Joe can't help making classic rock references, and Lady Cobra is described as someone with a 'black heart that beats crimson and clover.' Because she's significantly younger than him, he couldn't really write a love song to her or just describe her, so he sings funny lines like 'Do you wanna play a game of Twister like a dirty old man with a babysitter?' She just wants to be friends.

'Night Life' (Lyrics: Armstrong, Monica Painter; Music: Green Day)

One of the band's weakest tunes, 'Night Life', is considered to be so poor it's been a joke for Green Day fans for a decade now. Lady Cobra rapping was a turn-off for many, but at least the band were trying something new. There's a bit of a Clash rhythm in this, like on most of the *¡Dos!* songs, as it tries to lead garage rock into the 2010s, employing a touch of hip hop. This party song has little melody, no hook, and poor lyrics.

Billie Joe starts by describing a girl he likes. What else is new? Well, an actual woman responds, unlike every Green Day song ever (except for 'Letterbomb' with Kathleen Hanna). He has seen Lady Cobra in his nightlife. She responds that he shouldn't be shy and she'll take care of his needs. She also identifies herself as Nightlife. Whatever she sings, she's representing the seedy and shady side of partying. Billie Joe told MTV: 'This is the first collaboration in a long time. She's rapping. I'm the hype man.'

'Wow That's Loud' (Lyrics: Armstrong; Music: Green Day)

This plays as if Green Day were The Who in 1967, recording The Beatles 'She's A Woman.' It's one of Green Day's more-inspired efforts, and they give themselves some room to maneuver the dynamics. The ascending, stinging lead guitar slashes through with a tone that almost sounds like a vocal. They break in the middle for a cavernous psychedelic instrumental section that's a reminder of the adventurous psych breaks in some of The Yardbirds' best songs.

There are poppy Who/mod 'oooh' vocals, creating something totally new on the most-creative track of *¡Dos!* The guitar break finally shows Armstrong breaking free and jamming, losing track of the song before making his way back.

'Wow that dirty dress is so loud, and it goes...' cues the band to let loose and rock out to describe it instead of using words. The chorus seemingly starts awkwardly with 'Dressed to the nines like a black cat's eyes,' but it's a smart way of combining the cat adages with the heavy black eye shadow and flashy dress.

'Amy' (Lyrics: Armstrong, Music: Green Day)

This song was written as a tribute to the late British singer Amy Winehouse. The track comes at the end of the record like her passing meant the party was over; that her partying was over. 'Gone at 27 without a trace' was a reminder of other rock stars who died at 27, including Jimi Hendrix, Janis Joplin, Jim Morrison and Kurt Cobain. It's a sweet intimately-melodic tribute with a genuine, sincere vocal. 'Do you want to be a friend of mine?,' Armstrong inquires delicately over a gorgeous chord change before singing falsetto for the bridge. 'Amy' is a beautiful song that deserved more of a spotlight. Billie Joe commented on Amy's passing to *Billboard*: 'What she did – her knowledge of old music and old Motown – it's something in the chain of music, that is gone forever. She never got the help she needed. I know what it's like to go down a really dark path, and I have had good people around me to help me survive. Maybe that's why I was able to relate to her.'

¡Tré! (2012)

Personnel:
Billie Joe Armstrong: lead vocals, guitar, piano
Mike Dirnt: bass, backing vocals
Tré Cool: drums
Producers: Rob Cavallo, Green Day
Recorded at Jingletown Recording, Oakland, California
Label: Reprise
Release date: 7 December 2012
Charts: US: 13, UK: 31
Singles: 'X-Kid'

The pop-punk is fully back, but it's not like it once was long ago. Now it's more produced, less energetic, distorted and emotional. Cavallo's trilogy production has lacked spark, creativity and power. After *¡Tré!*, Cavallo was let go. The band unloaded 37 songs on the trilogy, and with fan stamina dwindling after two albums a few months apart, this third one struggled commercially. After the Billie Joe's iHeart Radio tantrum, followed by his going to rehab, the band moved the album's release forward to quash some of the controversy, but there was the prevailing feeling that they just wanted to wrap up the project fast and be done with it. Eventually, they admitted they could've been more selective. The band had written some weak, colorless songs that were mixed in with better tracks. On *¡Tré!*, they succeed with R&B on 'Brutal Love' (proving Billie Joe's desire to serve up resonant vocals was back), and they bring back the magic of their rock operas with 'Dirty Rotten Bastards' and the beautiful string-heavy 'The Forgotten.' The trilogy's gold nugget arrives in the song that features the most-perfect of everything: 'X-Kid.'

'Brutal Love' (Lyrics: Armstrong; Music: Green Day, Sam Cooke)
If Amy Winehouse's R&B had inspired Billie Joe, here we're treated to a melody from soul legend Sam Cooke's 'Bring It On Home To Me.' Cooke also died young when murdered in 1964. It's Green Day's first R&B song, using the horns and rhythms of 1960s soul. They mix 1950s-style guitar arpeggios with a 12/8 rhythm and plenty of harmonies. Armstrong removes all his aggression and attitude and does a tremendous job in R&B mode. Even his guitar solo that copies the melody, seems more inspired. Unfortunately, he added nothing to the melody, so it lacks the band's signature.
 'Brutal Love' is self-explanatory. Armstrong tells us how he defines the possible pitfalls of this brutal 'little thing called love,' but it's worth it. The chorus involving bitters and soda and 'bad love' is poorly written in another attempt to explain a love that's bittersweet. He told *Rolling Stone* he desired 'A sweeping feel like something you'd get on an old Otis Redding record.'

'Missing You' (Lyrics: Armstrong; Music: Green Day)

This is pretty typical of the trilogy as a whole. Based on a Mike Dirnt chord sequence, the track lacks the band's bite. Billie Joe's vocal renders little emotion, the rhythm never brings excitement or adventure, and the songwriting is a step or two down from typical Green Day quality. The hook and melody are alright – a bit better than many other trilogy songs – but the track blends in with mostly everything by reusing too many of the same ideas.

Billie Joe wakes up and realizes he can't live life properly without his love around – searching the moon for clues. Two people looking at the moon is a semi-common romantic song device.

'8th Avenue Serenade' (Lyrics: Armstrong; Music: Green Day)

There's nothing necessarily wrong with this song, but Mike and Tré keep retreading the same ground. It's fast, lacks aggression, and provides little power. Mike's 'ooh's lend some pop to the proceedings.

Billie Joe fears that his long-distance relationship will end. So if she leaves him, he'll look up at the stars and wonder where she is, just like he tried to 'search the moon' for the woman in 'Missing You.' The chorus better explains what's happening since he admits his imagination is getting carried away while he listens to music on 8th Avenue. In the verse two, he continues his minimal fare – 'Sing to me cradle songs for a midlife' acknowledges he's no longer hanging around with young people.

'Drama Queen' (Lyrics: Armstrong; Music: Green Day)

This shuffle ballad brings back the band's reliable melodic instincts. But as it continues its light piano rock with Armstrong on acoustic guitar, the melody rarely changes, so the constant recycling becomes tiresome. Without Mike or Tré working in their usual creative tricks, the song loses its luster.

The rich young 'Drama Queen' is profiled as a spoiled brat who 'dangles from her necklace.' She's all grown up and is 'old enough to bleed now.' The track was originally on the *¡Dos!* vinyl, but was switched to *¡Tré!*.

'X-Kid' (Lyrics: Armstrong; Music: Green Day)

This opening riff is one of the best riffs they've ever done, and the song has an amazing melody too. Possibly the trilogy's best track, 'X-Kid,' is enough to get a listener all tingly inside. The band sound energized, tight and muscular. Billie Joe sings wonderfully, like when he emotes, climbing the scale on the bridge. Even his guitar solo is one of the trilogy's best. It's exciting, lyrical, heroic, and emotional enough to match the nostalgia of the resonant lyrics. The bridge uses the melody of 'The Words I Might Have Ate.' It's clear that Green Day always perform better on the best compositions. Even Jason White's guitar part separates from Billie Joe's on the coda. The 'X-Kid' single could've charted higher if the fans weren't so worn out with 37 new songs to play within just a few months. *¡Dos!* sold just 165,000 copies, easily their worst sales since their indie rock days.

'Sex, Drugs & Violence' (Lyrics: Armstrong; Music: Green Day)
This song is a drop in quality. Armstrong and White use the same guitar tones and rhythmic feel they've used on most songs, and the solo uneventfully repeats the vocal melody. Mike provides solid harmony, but there's no threatening feeling of danger in the vocals. The song title makes one wonder why this wasn't on *¡Dos!*. But when you hear it, you realize it's one of the safest songs of their career. It holds a bland lyric about a high-school dropout whose life didn't work out because he didn't get a proper education.

'A Little Boy Named Train' (Lyrics: Armstrong; Music: Green Day)
Billie Joe's vocal lacks emotion, and the lyric lacks a stance, so it's hard to tell the intent. The instrumentation never budges from the same thing we've heard at least 15-20 times during this trilogy. The intro comes straight out of 'I Fought The Law.' At their best, the band can spice up a track, but the creeping feeling that they're on autopilot is hard to ignore.

This sad but true story about Billie Joe's son's classmate talks of the confusion in life when you're a castaway. Billie Joe said of the lyric: 'One of [Train's] parents was born a hermaphrodite, and [Train's parents] cut off the penis. The parents wanted the child to not be identified as a boy or a girl, and the child didn't really have a name; one week, it's Tigger, another it's Train. There's a line: 'I'm always lost, I'll never change/Give me directions and I'll get lost again.' Kind of autobiographical.'

'Amanda' (Lyrics: Armstrong; Music: Green Day)
'Amanda' finds Billie Joe singing happily as if he doesn't know the lyric is sad. On the guitar break, he does a great job of injecting character into the playing, breaking through the soft-edged production momentarily.

The famous rebel ex-girlfriend 'Amanda' is back, and Billie Joe is more direct and personal than on any other song he wrote about her. He knows they weren't meant to be together, but wants to say hello after so long, remembering her fondly.

'Walk Away' (Lyrics: Armstrong; Music: Green Day)
After a quiet opening, we're into slightly different territory on this disappointing power ballad that borrows Pete Townshend riffs from The Who's 'Baba O'Reilly.' At least the feel differs from other tracks, but the guitar tones are still too weak to break through the safe pop/rock production. Billie Joe sings happily, but perhaps too happily, since it uses a tongue-in-cheek answer to difficult world problems. It's a simple song about walking away from a no-win situation, licking your wounds, remembering the scars and moving forward with life. It was supposedly one of the lost tracks from the

Cigarettes and Valentines project. It's one of the band's least original tracks, and one of their most-boring.

'Dirty Rotten Bastards' (Lyrics: Armstrong; Music: Green Day)

This song, in five parts, is the trilogy's longest, and the story overlaps both of the band's rock operas. In Part I, Billie Joe calls a therapy session gathering all the 'retarded and brokenhearted' to remind them that they're the hypnotized sheep of society. The happy harmonies over the large guitar lines go a long way to satisfy, by adding some color, which also hides the verse melody being recycled from 'Brat.'

After a brief solo bass interlude, Part II ups the energy and keeps the power. Armstrong – by then in his 40s – claims he and the others are too old to party. With full distortion, this is one of their most inspired efforts. All four members are on fire and really light up *¡Tré!* with sonic fireworks and a dirty, raw vibe like that of 'Makeout Party.'

Part III finds Armstrong deciding the crew should revolt against those who are using them for personal gain. He meets Juliana Homicide – someone who can encourage him to cause a disruption in the system through violent means. It's the most melodic section, and the melody is enhanced. Billie Joe has some of the it factor that made him so resonant with his audience. Like their other epics, they end in a group sing-along for a big final chorus of 'carried away.'

The pre-chorus has the narrator on a path of destruction. Part IV just repeats the verse and chorus from part I, indicating that nothing's really changed and they're still living in the 'season of misery.' Part V consists of the 'we're carried away' section. They destroyed a city for nothing. It also retreads ground extensively covered on their rock operas. It stands as the trilogy's most accomplished and creative song; one that sits well with their 2000s work. Billie Joe told *The Sun*: '('Dirty Rotten Bastards' is) an arena song, then a sing-along, and it takes off. We wanted to make something similar to 'Jesus Of Suburbia' or the B-side of The Beatles' *Abbey Road*. It's a number of songs combined that make a giant sing-along and something you can dance to.'

'99 Revolutions' (Lyrics: Armstrong; Music: Green Day)

'We are the 99%' was a phrase used by the political Occupy movements in the early 2010s to signify that 99% of the US population were suffering financially. Green Day transported that theory into '99 Revolutions': one of the trilogy's few explicitly-political songs. 'There's a 'Going out of business' sale and a race to bankruptcy' recalls all of the small businesses leaving town, overtaken by large corporations or greedy landlords, resulting in cities becoming homogenized. The sentiment is simple – the 99% need help, and the world spins 99 times but not 100 – metaphorically representing Green Day's view. Many in the US think that the top 1%'s wealth is highly disproportionate compared to the rest of the population. The philosophy claims that 99%

of people are living their lives on a revolving planet controlled by that top 1%. The band loved the song, named the tour with the title, and felt inspired by the sentiment. While the melodic verses work well, the chorus has little melody, there's no hook at all, and the title feels like it's repeated 99 times.

Armstrong told *Rolling Stone* about how they wanted to participate in the 99% movement: 'We wanted to be part of it in some way. I thought it was about working people and where we come from. But Oakland got really complicated when the anarchists started coming in. I'm not into that – smashing the windows in a small business.'

'The Forgotten' (Lyrics: Armstrong; Music: Green Day)

We've made it all the way to the trilogy's final song: the epic 'The Forgotten.' It's a grand statement with a sweeping string arrangement and easily one of the best melodies of the trilogy. Hearing Billie Joe using the best beautiful voice he can find is another indicator that some songs meant more to him than others. Everything works here, from the piano to the memorable guitar solo – reflective and searching amidst the orchestral backdrop.

The song is about those who are ignored or cast aside and never heard from by the general public. He thinks their spirit guided them to a forgotten space because they were 'losing their faith to their abandon.' The pre-chorus changes from third to second-person to tell us, 'Well don't look away from the arms of a bad dream/Don't look away/'Cause sometimes you're better lost than seen.'

The beautiful second verse finds Billie Joe reflective, trying to explain that they're like soldiers of a lost war; invisible to the rest of society. It's an excellent sequence, which continues for the main chorus. He requests that we don't look away from a moment, the future, and from love. It's a lovely sentiment, completing the 37-song trilogy.

Related Tracks

'State Of Shock' can be found under *Demolicious*.

¡Cuatro! (2013)

The documentary for ¡Uno!,¡Dos!, and Tré! has the band in the studio rehearsing the songs. The majority of the trilogy songs are included, usually heard in excerpts, and we visit each of the recording locations for band rehearsals. The biggest revelation is that Billie Joe's guitar is in the left channel throughout the trilogy, and Jason White's in the right, making it easy to hear White's only contributions to the band's albums. 'Amy' and 'Walk Away' appear in instrumental form, though neither recording was issued.

Demolicious (Compilation) (2014)

A compilation of trilogy demos and one leftover. But the compilation has a shoddy reputation.

'State of Shock' (Lyrics: Armstrong; Music: Green Day)

This fast garage rocker being issued here in its raw form doesn't necessarily help it. The melody sounds like a mix of early Who and the Green Day song 'Chump,' and the instrumentation is cymbal-happy but otherwise standard. It starts with the narrator wondering about his health. He thinks he's going to die, but the uplifting chorus is there to soothe him. It talks of people who are their deathbeds, scared to die, even though throughout their lives they said they wanted to go to heaven. One humorous moment comes when Billie sings, 'My tears are putting out my cigarette/I'm singing out the alphabet the way I remember/Should I be concerned?' It's funny because he sang the same lines on 'Angel Blue' on *¡Uno!,* but then claims his memory is shoddy as a result of amnesia.

'X-Mas Time Of Year' (Lyrics: Armstrong; Music: Green Day)

On one of Green Day's classiest songs, Armstrong sings a sweet lyric that can skip along happily. It's a humble song that appreciates the time of year and loved ones. It sounds like his voice is effected to sound lighter and smaller than usual. He may not have gotten a hit out of this, but it sounds like he tried, displaying his undying sense of melody. Tré stays relaxed, and Mike lays out a complementary bass line to underscore the optimism.

Revolution Radio (2016)

Personnel:
Billie Joe Armstrong: lead vocals, guitar, piano
Mike Dirnt: bass, backing vocals
Tré Cool: drums, percussion
Additional personnel:
Ronnie Blake: trumpet ('Bouncing Off The Wall')
Producer: Green Day
Recorded at OTIS, Oakland, California
Label: Reprise/Warner Bros.
Release date: 7 October 2016
Charts: US: 1, UK: 1
Singles: 'Bang Bang,' 'Still Breathing,' 'Revolution Radio'

The grand return of the Green Day we all know and love, *Revolution Radio* not only improved on their last few albums, but it may be their fourth-best album behind *Dookie, American Idiot* and *Kerplunk*. Producing themselves, they came up with incredible songs and dynamics that remind fans of the 2000s era. But this album is more accessible because the songs function individually without a storyline.

The album was a big success, hitting number 1 in the US, and the singles 'Bang Bang' and 'Still Breathing' topped the rock chart. Green Day earned back their reputation just after being inducted into the Rock and Roll Hall of Fame in 2015.

Billy Joe is back to his excellent lyrics, alternating between politics and nostalgia, and the band perform like they're hungry again. Critics and fans were happy once again.

'Somewhere Now' (Lyrics: Armstrong; Music: Green Day)

'Somewhere Now' is brilliant all around. It easily tops every song from the trilogy, and may be their best song since *American Idiot*. The quality control had taken multiple steps up.

It opens with heavenly acoustic guitar and soft touches of whispering guitar volume swells, deftly adding depth to the sparse sound. Billie Joe sings sweetly until midway into the final verse line, when his voice changes upon the band building up behind. Then the band fully enter, finding a fresh rock rhythm that Armstrong rides on until they reach the upbeat arena-rock 'all die in threes' section. Half a minute later, that dies down and harmonies arise, Billie Joe singing the title with a slight filter effect. The quiet is just a setup for a colossal rhythm that could set fire to a radio like on the album cover. They're using Who dynamics, with crushing drums, emphatic-but-intelligent bass, and cataclysmic guitar, fueling one of the band's all-time greatest arrangements and performances.

The protagonist is scrambling to get out the door. He's getting ready to go into the future, 'Where the future promises ain't what they used to be.'

Then he sings about his life being mild when it used to be wild. 'I put the riot in patriot and we all die in threes' continues the brilliance, and Billie Joe's wordplay is back in action. He was formerly a Whatsername-type rebel, but now is just hypnotized by mainstream media, medicated by doctors, and artificially serene. In verse two, this rambunctious former rebel has 'A seat in the middle of the road,' and shops 'online so I can vote.' 'Hallelujah, I found my soul underneath the sofa pillows/Congratulations, I found myself somewhere now,' he sings sardonically. .

'Bang Bang' (Lyrics: Armstrong; Music: Green Day)
The brutal 'Bang Bang' is one of their biggest bangers and one of their most powerful performances ever. The dizzying, turbocharged rhythm is practically impossible to keep steady and consistent, but they tame this monster. In 'Bang Bang' the narrator is the shooter, which can be difficult to pull off properly. Billie Joe suggests that it's not just about murder, hate and revenge, but an easy way to become a 'celebrity.' 'Daddy's little psycho, mommy's little soldier' he sings on the chorus, as if his parents are proud of his murderous actions. He claims he's a hero, like many who think they're securing justice for a violent minority willing to commit terrorist acts. 'Bang bang gimme fame/Shoot me up to entertain/I am a semiautomatic lonely boy.' Armstrong told *Rolling Stone*:

> 'Bang Bang' is about racist police brutality involving guns, gun control in general, and mass shootings. All three were prevalent topics in the 2010s and 2020s, and Green Day wanted to take an anti-violent stance. It's about the culture of mass shooting that happens in America, mixed with narcissistic social media. There's this sort-of rage happening, but it's also now being filmed, and we all have ourselves under surveillance. After I wrote it, all I wanted to do was get that out of my brain because it just freaked me out.

'Revolution Radio' (Lyrics: Armstrong; Music: Green Day)
Inspired by Black Lives Matter protests, 'Revolution Radio' discusses strained US race relations in the late-2010s. There were nationwide cases of police murdering black people and taking justice into their own hands – in the age of cell phones, and witnesses able to make videos and send them to the press to help identify guilty police parties. The nation felt like they were witnessing things for the first time, though racist police brutality had been going on for years. Billie Joe told *Rolling Stone*: 'I was screaming, 'Hands up, don't shoot.' I felt like I was on the right side of history. They really don't know what the African-American experience truly is. When you have people getting shot in their cars for no reason, and being put in jail cells for profit, we have a serious problem, and the first thing you need to do is get educated.' Billie Joe saw the dehumanization of the police, singing 'life has been deleted,' like a black person was a computer file to discard.

Verse two talks of racial protesting and the tear gas police and government officials used in the 1960s and 2010s. 'But the air is barely breathing' is a terrific lyrical turn that can be linked to cigarette seller and murder victim Eric Garner, who screamed 'I can't breathe' over and over. He died as a result of a police officer's illegal chokehold on him for selling single cigarettes on the street without a license.

Memories of *American Idiot* flood-in with 'The dawn of the new airwaves for the anti-social media', playing on social media and how people use it to be hateful while attempting to dispel news stories. Armstrong felt it was time to stand up and fight like his fictional characters of the past. A siren guitar effect open's the track before the band rip apart the police station with blazing guitars, destructive drumming and a colossal bass tones. This is just what the doctor ordered – Green Day with all the energy and stamina they had in the 1990s.

'Say Goodbye' (Lyrics: Armstrong; Music: Green Day)
This continues the anti-violent trip as the detailing of America's problems continue. 'Bang Bang' was a sarcastic take on violence, while this song is humble, discussing the resulting depression, despair and anger as victims and their loved ones say goodbye to the world that treated them unfairly.

The band successfully branch out here with newer production techniques heard in the way the beats are artificially pumped up, the distant harmonies and the busy percussion. Everything shoots out of the speakers in a massive way – even Armstrong's curled whirls of distortion and Tré's ear-bleeding bass drum. Armstrong's vocal sounds fully invested, like he is on the entire album. Mostly everything is fresh and new.

'Teach your children well from the bottom of a well' is a winking line that sums up some of Michigan's urban issues, with poor-quality drinking water being one of the major concerns.

The police and violence are passing topics in this song that prioritizes remembering loved ones and all the unfortunate people that passed away under horrific conditions, whether due to violence, environment or hate.

'Outlaws' (Lyrics: Armstrong; Music: Green Day)
The stadium-sized, 21st-century arena-rock production can fit the endearing rocker 'Say Goodbye' or the sweet and reflective 'Outlaws.' The beautiful melody would be a bigger feather in Green Day's cap if it didn't so closely resemble Electric Light Orchestra's 'Can't Get It Out Of My Head'. The two intro's of both can be a future mashup since the chords, vocal melody and drums start up all in the exact same way. When Green Day reach the chorus, Armstrong adds his iteration of Jeff Lynne's musical piece, and as a combined forced, the two push 'Outlaws' to be the album's most melodic song.

The song describes the band's sneaky, snarky, mischievous ways. Billie Joe gets personal, linking him and his band to delinquency, acquiring scars from crazy stunts, breaking hearts, trying to hotwire cars and setting off bottle rockets. It closes with a train leaving a station, like the one in 'Christie Road' – as a euphonism for Green Day, leaving the past and living for the future.

'Bouncing Off The Wall' (Lyrics: Armstrong; Music: Green Day)
The band's self-production turns this track into something fresher. The modern production sheen spotlights Armstrong's splendid singing.

The song might as well have been sung by St. Jimmy from *American Idiot,* as this protagonist wants to drive fast through life with the Devil by his side; upset by the Government, the radio and everything else that feels oppressing. 'Radio covered in gasoline' portrays the album cover as an anti-media statement.

'Still Breathing' (Lyrics: Armstrong; Music: Green Day, Richard Parkhouse, Adam Slack, Luke Spiller, George Tizzard, Joshua Wilkinson)
This brilliant song is one of the band's best late works because it harnesses all the real emotion of Armstrong's substance abuse, and produces another amazing uplifter. Usually, when he writes a song close to his personal life, the audience doesn't know the background unless he tells them. With this highly-melodic tune, he's singing about recovering from his emotional breakdown that aired live during the infamous iHeart Radio concert played to promote *¡Uno!*. This was Armstrong's way of finding closure with the public and his fans. He triumphantly sings like he's conquered his problems and, therefore, the world's, or at least those in *his* world. Though his voice strains some, the song calls for just these exact notes, and it paid off. It was the album's second *Billboard* rock-chart number one single.

Everyone gets knocked down. What matters is how you get up. Billie Joe inhabits the lives of several folks who are going through the good and the bad of life. He equates himself to people and things, indicating life's roller coaster. He then sings the chorus as an inspiration to others that he's still alive and breathing – 'My head's above the rain and roses' indicating he's not ready for his funeral just yet. In 2016, he told *Rolling Stone*: 'It goes from the life of a junkie to the life of a gambler to the life of a single mother and a soldier, and how we're all kinda intertwined. Sometimes I run away from being too heavy. But sometimes it just comes out that way.' He included a couplet about being raised without his father, by a mother who was 'barely keepin' it together': the truthful element within the song's fiction.

'Youngblood' (Lyrics: Armstrong; Music: Green Day)
With group chants of 'Youngblood' opening the song, new arrangements, song structures and sounds come into the material. The average songwriting is here upped by the time and effort put into the performance and production. There's a hook, a pretty bridge and a bright energy that sounds

like the work of someone 20 years younger, but a poor lyric. Billie Joe wrote it for his wife, Adrienne. 'She's a loner, not a stoner'; 'She's the cedar in the trees of Minnesota'; 'She's my weakness' and 'She's my little youngblood.' There are some awkward lines that seem forced, hindering the song some. Armstrong implied this was a song from the scrapped 2003 project *Cigarettes and Valentines*.

'Too Dumb To Die' (Lyrics: Armstrong; Music: Green Day)
This may be the closest the band come to their 1990s sound. With just some added group backing vocals, a great riff dividing chorus from verse and some handclaps, they freshen that old sound for the 2010s to great effect. The song itself isn't bad, but the performance overshadows it.

The odd phrase 'Too dumb to die' was already used in 'Sex Drugs & Violence.' Here, it means the band's dreams to make a living as musicians. It's a brief autobiography, beginning when they were teens running amok, skipping school, smoking dope and causing trouble like outlaws. 'I feel like a cello lost over the rainbow' was an odd line representing sadness. Verse two veers into talk about his father and his union for his job. Like his father, Billie Joe was looking for a cause, and found music. He told NPR: 'That is more personal. It's about growing up totally working-class and not knowing what the future was going to be, and being sort of a dope-smoking kid. And then it's also a reference to my father, who was in the Teamsters.'

'Troubled Times' (Lyrics: Armstrong; Music: Green Day)
'Troubled Times' stays in the *Revolution Radio* sonic orbit but drifts towards a *21st Century Breakdown* sound. Mike's succulent bass line leads the quiet verses, and the chorus is led by the fine guitars and terrific melody. Tré's chorus cymbal crashes, up the intensity on contrast with the chaotic nature of troubled times. The verses serve as the peaceful time when it's okay to lick the wounds.

After a nostalgia trip lightens the mood of the earlier heavy political songs, the album picks back up on the political trail, summoning strength for another round against this wicked planet. 'What good is love and peace on Earth when it's exclusive?' Billie Joe starts by talking about class and race structure, then confesses on behalf of those around him that they don't read the news anyway; they just make up their own truths. In the next verse, he offers the wise philosophy that people won't improve and grow empathetic if they don't try or care anyway. 'We run for cover like a skyscraper's falling down' reminds us that the US has been at war almost since the beginning of the 21st century.

'Forever Now' (Lyrics: Armstrong; Music: Green Day)
The overtly personal nature of some of the album's songs contrast heavily with what's come before. In the past, Armstrong would hide personal

elements behind frustrated narrators and characters, but here he comes right out like he's at an AA meeting.

'Part I: I'm Freaking Out' opens the mammoth track which is broken into three parts. It's adventurous, melodic, exciting and everything that was great about Green Day in the 2000s. They sound unafraid to search for gold, and they strike it rich with amazing individual efforts instrumentally: especially Tré. The complex structure has them running through their own obstacle course, coming out with a grandiose statement. They succeed mightily. When the track comes around to the 'Somewhere Now' reprise, they even provide a fresh take on that song's melody. The Who continue to have a big influence on these epics, but Green Day have restocked their sonic supermarket with fresh, new and stimulating foods to nourish their fans forever.

'My name is Billie, and I'm freaking out/I thought, therefore I was/Well I can't really figure it out,' plays off the Descartes phrase 'I think, therefore I am.' 'Scream out my memories as if I was never there' is another way of telling the audience that many of the songs that don't appear to be personal, really *are* – not all, but many. Armstrong said the same about *21st Century Breakdown* and how its characters were just extensions of his own personality.

The confessional continues in verse two with lines straight out of his mind, void of the usual poetry. He wonders why he had to work to be 'born this way,' and why life didn't feel more natural. He quit school but was able to shine playing his guitar.

In 'Part II: A Better Way to Die,' Billie Joe goes on about how revolution looks for escape, as the band continue on a sonic high. In 'Part III: Somewhere Now (Reprise),' he brings it all home as he wonders why he's rushing off to another obligation he's not interested in. At the end, he changes the 'Somewhere Now' line from 'How did life on the wild side ever get so *dull*?' been '*full*'. He's learned that life is so much more than what kids and teens think. He told *Rolling Stone*:

'Forever Now' brings it full-circle, and honestly, it's so fun to write like that. You can just be that little kid in your room and feeling like a rock god. It begins with a lyric, 'My name is Billie and I'm freaking out,' is the most honest line I've ever written, and ends with the refrain, 'I ain't gonna stand in line no more.' It's like a slogan for a demonstration, like, 'I'm not going to accept the status quo' or 'I'm not going to be manipulated.' But at the end, when we bring in that big chorus where everything is overlapping with each other and heading back into that riff, it was just fucking beautiful.

'Ordinary World' (Lyrics: Armstrong; Music: Green Day)

This one final sweet, quiet and humble moment wraps up *Revolution Radio*. Written for the film of the same name, the protagonist wants to be a rock star, but hasn't found success. Billie Joe knows how to sing, and had been emoting differently on all of their 21st-century albums. He no longer needs an attitude for a vocal if the song doesn't need it. He sings quietly, sweetly and with rich emotion. He plays the one instrument on the song: an acoustic guitar.

The song theorizes about what life might've been if things hadn't worked out with Green Day. He mentions the 'city of shining light,' which is a heavily-populated city like the 'city of lights' found in 'Are We The Waiting.' It asks questions about life, but finds no answers. Billie Joe wonders what it's like to be a star, and what he'd do. He sings he'd walk to the end of the Earth, just like he was on the edge of the world in 'Forever Now.' 'Baby, I don't have much/But what we have is more than enough/Ordinary world.' Without the taste of stardom Green Day had, Armstrong thinks he would not need fame and could settle down in a nice, humble family with a loving wife.

Greatest Hits: God's Favorite Band (2017)

Green Day's second greatest-hits album covers their entire career,and features a fine alternate version of 'Ordinary World' with singer Miranda Lambert, and has the new 'Back In The USA'

'Back In The USA' (Lyrics: Armstrong; Music: Green Day)

Here the bigger *Revolution Radio* sound powers a track that's almost as good as the hits it sits with on the compilation. *With* Mike's added harmonies, the anthemic chorus is highly satisfying.

Usually, we've found Billie Joe awakening in his bedroom – when he includes mundane, everyday details of his protagonist – but this time, he's waking up on high, stormy seas, riding one he calls 'Noah's Ark.' He sees riot gear everywhere as if he's in the Navy and coming home from war. But when he sees a parade as he gets back to the USA, it's not a homecoming for war veterans, but a parade of supporters for US President Donald Trump. 'Let freedom ring with all the crazies on parade/Let them eat poison/It tastes like lemonade.' Armstrong is giving an account of a war veteran's shock when they see how the country changes.

The chorus talks more about the parade to re-emphasize that the narrator was at war. In the next verse, he stresses how feeling safe at home is another way of letting chaos reign. And again, the choice of acting or laying low and out of trouble is considered.

Father of All Motherf**kers (2020)

Personnel:
Billie Joe Armstrong: lead vocals, guitar
Mike Dirnt: bass, backing vocals
Tré Cool: drums, percussion
Producers: Butch Walker, Chris Dugan, Green Day
Recorded at Hyde Street, San Francisco, California
Label: Reprise
Release date: 7 February 2020
Charts: US: 4, UK: 1
Singles: 'Father of All Motherf**ckers,' 'Oh Yeah'

Green Day want to dance. There's a lot of dance-pop on the airwaves currently, and the band merely adjust their sound by adding more garage rock, percussion, and particularly handclaps. But this dance rock is pretty heavily politicized. Though most political references are purposely vague and general, the combination of dance and politics could've been successful, but there are some issues. They are significant enough for fans to wonder if it was only a contractual obligation record, since it's the last of the Reprise contract. Some of the problems come from the band's overall philosophy. Punk fans don't usually want to dance, so it's tough for them to transition into happy-sounding rhythm-oriented dance rock. Fans had to wait four years for a 26-minute album. The title track and 'Oh Yeah' were both top-10 US Rock-chart singles, but they were not loved as much as prior singles.

The band sound has lost the adventurous dynamics of the trilogy, so it's up to the songwriting to pull the heavy load. Yet, they don't reach the high peaks of their previous work. Another problem from the trilogy comes back to haunt them, in the vocal department. While Billie Joe was working with new falsetto vocals, he was losing his resonance and emotion. With happy music and sad lyrics on most songs, it's as if he doesn't know which way to go, so there's no vocal emotion either way. Unfortunately, it's been a rough start for Green Day in the 2020s, with many fans unsatisfied with *Father of All*. Critics were kinder, but no one would confuse this album with the band's best. On the bright side, there are still some fine melodies and hooks, and it's somewhat refreshing to hear happy music. Billie Joe told *Spin* in 2020:

> I think this whole record, the point was to make Green Day more danceable. So songs like 'Meet Me On The Roof' or 'Father of All,' those are the two songs I think of where you can. The first video we made for this, we were showing all of these different images of people dancing, whether it was kids break dancing or kids doing a wall of death, and just sort of that common natural instinct with beats that make people want to move.

He told *NME* in 2020: 'You can't help but think about Trump a little bit, but that wasn't really in the front of my mind. Father Of All Motherfuckers is just a badass title. It was just too obvious. We live in really dangerous times right now. Everything feels sort of unpredictable. America is really fucked up, and it's hard to draw any inspiration from it, because it depresses me.'

'Father of All Motherfuckers' (Lyrics: Armstrong; Music: Green Day)

It's clear from the very first electronically-processed falsetto vocal that the band are continuing their updated production. They add some adventurous stereo guitar effects, and additional percussion to better emphasize the beat (including handclaps) on top of the pop-punk/garage-rock mix they began with Foxboro Hot Tubs. Billie Joe tackles Trump's denial of the world's environmental concerns, and worries that if the people at the top ignore it, we have no defense. Armstrong discussed 'Lyin' in a bed of blood and money' with radio host Howard Stern: 'This is the first time I talked about money. I have mixed emotions about it – the imposter syndrome or something like that. We come from such broke backgrounds. For me, it's been a trip.' Armstrong explained to *Rolling Stone*:

I was getting deep into Motown and soul music, and trying to channel that. I'd been listening to the first couple of Prince records, and everything is in falsetto. At the same time, I was in this weird kind of depression, and that's what the song is about. With Trump, it's this toxicity that's in our culture, and we're deeply, deeply divided to a point of paranoia that we've never felt before. There's a line: 'We are rivals in the riot that's inside of us.' I feel like that's what's happening in our culture.

'Fire, Ready, Aim' (Lyrics: Armstrong; Music: Green Day)

Here they mix the dance elements with piano. It jumps around, discussing kicking a dog, lying, hyperbole and whistleblowing, which can be projected onto the US government when it comes to politician scandals. According to Billie Joe, a powerful politician hears that a whistleblower in his camp, ratted him out. The person is fired, and the lying and hyperbole to the press, begins. Verse two shows the band's frustration with all the lying and false information. They left a description of the song under its YouTube video: 'This song is about our daily outrage. Attack without thought, hyperbole. Anyway, stick a hammer in your mouth. Shut up and dance!'

'Oh Yeah' (Lyrics: Armstrong; Music: Green Day)

This track shares its time between a garage, dance club and a 1980s-throwback new-wave party. There's no attitude or aggression since it has an uplifting spirit, but Armstrong doesn't seem fully invested when he sings pessimistic lyrics. And the 'Oh yeah' chorus chant leans into the irony

127

of a happy song with a sad lyric. Joan Jett's 'Do You Wanna Touch Me? (Oh Yeah)' was used as a sample: inspiring the song title.

Billie Joe plays the bad guy – like he's done on many songs – and in verse one, he has forced a crowd of protestors onto the dirt with their hands up: presumably in his role as a police officer. 'Everybody is a star' symbolizes Armstrong's thoughts on no one taking selfies at protests, using more pessimism than when Sly and the Family Stone sang 'Everybody Is A Star' in 1969. Armstrong told *Kerrang!*: 'It's a way to say that being part of a protest or movement is not about going on YouTube, Instagram or Snapchat to make yourself a star, but about being part of something bigger than yourself.' To him, it's another facetious way of portraying a rotten situation since some use social media for popularity with optimism. Green Day are saying it as a pessimistic refrain.

Verse three sees the policeman – who doesn't believe in knowledge – burning books from his backpack. The song's working title was 'Bulletproof Backpack'. The narrator feels books teach unruly individualism. Billy Joe told *Kerrang!*: 'It's sort of about being freaked out by the polarization that we live in right now. Whether it's kids getting shot in schools or the closest thing that America has ever seen to fascism.'

'Meet Me On The Roof' (Lyrics: Armstrong; Music: Green Day)
This grower takes a few listens to sink in, but once it does, it's an emphatic, fun dance-rock number with light funk guitar licks, happy singing, great harmonies and an actual contentment with life very rarely heard in the Green Day catalog. They visit the garage for tougher guitar licks and that 1960s organ sound, then work on their synchronized handclaps.

The reminiscing here includes a woman in a window, who Billie Joe wants just like in the band's very first number '1000 Hours.' But his face feels numb like it did on *Insomniac*'s 'Geek Stink Breath.' He feels unworthy of the woman, like he did so many times before, and asks for forgiveness, and 'How high is your low gonna go, girl?' The song is a playful, youthful romance that alleviates the heavy topics of the first three songs. Tré told *Spin* in 2020: 'I think it's got a really sweet sentiment, but it's also got sort-of a cool toughness about it, and the vibe is really positive and it sounds classic in a way.'

'I Was A Teenage Teenager' (Lyrics: Armstrong; Music: Green Day)
After a full solo Billie Joe introduction verse, the band still feel those good vibes from 'Meet Me On The Roof,' mixing aggressive slashing rhythmic moments with a cool mid-tempo groove. The brash, bold chorus is catchy, and lots of vocals make it feel like the band are in agreement, especially since they *were* all together causing trouble as teens.

The nostalgia trip they took on *Revolution Radio*, continues. Armstrong writes a clearheaded lyric about feeling like a sourpuss as a teen, losing the drugs his friends asked him to hold, and not liking school. He sings, 'Living like a prisoner for haters,' inferring his mindset from 'Longview', where he locked the door to his own cell and lost the key. He remembers punishing himself for feeling crazy and not like others when it came to romance, drugs or school.

Mike Dirnt told *Playboy*:

I was a (Teenage Teenager). I was terribly stubborn. And as for the girls, hey, I didn't get it right. They just didn't want to meet me. The youth was a constant struggle; a constant feeling of inadequacy.' Tré Cool added: 'I was a frustrated, searching, sometimes happy teenager. The three of us were the outsiders – the freaks, not the least bit crazy.' Armstrong added: 'I wanted to write a song about what it is like to grow up as an ordinary guy. There are so many extreme teenagers in art.

'Stab You In The Heart' (Lyrics: Armstrong; Music: Green Day)
Like a failed attempt at recreating the garage rock of *¡Dos!*, this has attitude, with sweeping pissed guitar and tough drumming, but leaves behind melody, ambition and great lyrics. It's about a woman who betrays Billie Joe by going naked and telling lies in a porn magazine. He wants revenge, but it has no heart – it's just a quick summary and an empty-sounding threat. Tré told *Spin* in 2020: 'Stab You In The Heart' is really fun to play live. It's a barn-burning rock-and-roll extravaganza with murderous undertones.'

'Sugar Youth' (Lyrics: Armstrong; Music: Green Day)
At under two minutes, 'Sugar Youth' is another happy, danceable track. The party lyric matches the tempo and atmosphere, but it's more of the same.

The narrator wants to get wasted on 'yayo' – a mix of cocaine and sugar – and is jumping off the walls because he needs another fix. 'Sugar Youth' explains that people need to escape from the world's issues. As a side note, the line "Mano Y Mano' on the stereo and there ain't a cure' refers to the *uncool* 1970s/1980s act Hall and Oates and their hit 'Mano A Mano.' The establishment favored Hall and Oates, while the 1980s indie world favored cool act The Cure. Both acts are in the Rock and Roll Hall of Fame. It serves as a metaphor that shows Billie Joe favors those against the establishment.

'Junkies On A High' (Lyrics: Armstrong; Music: Green Day)
This comedown arrives after the high of 'Sugar Youth,' and Billie Joe sounds appropriately tired – the first time he changes his generally-happy mood. The band has calmed as well, feeling worn out and losing their identity. Anybody could be behind this slow groove wrapped in a 2020s production, but the little sound effects keep the sound fresh.

Using the 'Sugar Youth' narrator, Armstrong uses drugs as a way to escape. He sings about watching the world burn while living it up, and he identifies as 'Nobody,' like he did in '21st Century Breakdown' when he was 'no one.' It's one of the band's most prevalent lyrical themes. In the chorus, Armstrong mentions being 'another rock 'n' roll tragedy.' He told *Spin* in 2020: 'I think that line kind of scared me. I think the track record of rock musicians living short lives, sometimes it feels like hell hounds on your trail a little bit.'

'Take The Money And Crawl' (Lyrics: Armstrong; Music: Green Day)

After a brief, dramatic Wild West showdown-style opening, the band gradually work their way into the song, and it's really them this time – back to a more-identifiable sound that remains new. Adding a bit of garage, dance rock and more harmonies, they come through with a more powerful statement.

The original title, 'Art Of The Deal With The Devil' was changed to twist the common phrase 'take the money and run.' Armstrong linked Donald Trump's book title *The Art of the Deal,* with the expression 'Deal with the Devil.' It seems like another conscious decision to hold back what they really want to say. Another song title comes up in the verse one lines 'Sweet soul sickness/ Can I get a witness.' 'Can I Get A Witness' was a 1963 hit for soul legend Marvin Gaye.

'Take The Money And Crawl' is made up of short, pessimistic, three-word lines indicating that the protagonist's life sucks; he's a nasty guy and is willing to hurt others or do nefarious things for money, with no conscience.

'Graffitia' (Lyrics: Armstrong; Music: Green Day)

Unfortunately, yet again Green Day play the melody from 'I Fought The Law': a song they covered in 2004. Luckily, they add a second strong melody for the chorus, making sure they go out on a high. Like all the songs, it's another low-ambition dance-rock number that shines some sun rays into a new decade with a fresh and optimistic point of view. While the lyric mixes optimism and pessimism, the music remains upbeat.

The first pre-chorus (which starts the song) deals with the Rust Belt and miners losing jobs, while the second one is about blacks being shot by Chicago police. The chorus asks if the victims are 'the forgotten' – referencing the band's 2012 song – and the 'long lost love.' Armstrong changes the meaning to refer to these victims as the love we've lost in society. The 'perfect crime' in 'Graffitia' is getting rid of those considered of a lower economic class. Billie Joe told *Playboy*: 'The political content is still there, but it's more subtle.'

Non-album singles

'Dreaming' (Deborah Harry, Chris Stein)

This was released as a stand-alone single in May 2020. Like their other covers, the trio came up with a solid offering, but it can't be regarded as the definitive version.

'Here Comes The Shock' (Green Day)

This non-LP single was released in February 2021. Armstrong's vocal is reloaded with the emotion missing from *Father of All*. It's a shame the refrain is repeated so much.

This song could've fit into one their rock operas. The protagonist gathers a gang for a revolution. 'We are the broken records sitting in the sun' is a great line acknowledging that protestors repeat chants just like a record that's warped from sitting in the sun too long. The rest is written with generalized threats, but amongst the highlights is the line 'screaming bloody murder' reused from 'Ashley,' the *Annie Get Your Gun* movie reference, and 'Be-bop-a-lula': the title of the 1956 Gene Vincent song. It also references the 1996 film *Rumble in the Streets*, about a renegade policeman who murders the homeless – tying right into Green Day's themes of the past. They color the otherwise-standard lyric.

'Polyanna' (Green Day)

After working on Blondie's 'Dreaming,' perhaps new wave was still on their mind when they brought in an early-1980s synthesizer from a music store, and weaved it into the optimistic sound of this great inspirational song. Like many acts in the 2010s, Green Day allowed for some 1980s influence, creating a danceable pop/rock number that lacks aggressive playing. Dirnt and Cool lay low for the most part, only getting worked up for 'Hey' vocal backing and a bit more rhythmic intensity on the chorus.

The band's second straight stand-alone single, 'Polyanna,' was released in May 2021. Their career has been filled with pessimism, but there are some shining sprinkles of hope mixed in. When they go for the motivational song, they usually succeed mightily, as is the case here. Armstrong is singing and writing from the heart – telling listeners to stay strong, don't give up hope, be kind to others, and believe the truth and not whatever opinion best fits your needs. On the bridge, he reaffirms that it's worth being nice to others and sharing your love. 'Pollyanna' is a description for an optimistic person.

'Rock And Roll All Nite' (Live from Hella Mega)

Live from their Hella Mega Tour in 2021; this 1970s kiss hit is a standard affair – just a fun song played with Green Day flair. It was issued as a standalone track in 2021.

'Holy Toledo!' (Green Day)

Green Day discover the Arctic Monkeys, Franz Ferdinand and others from rock's most-recent major movement: the post-punk 2000s and the New York scene. The beats are hopped up, the bass and drums are tight, and the keyboard lays out like bedding underneath the bright rhythm and enthusiastic vocals. Green Day's fourth straight standalone single, 'Holy Toledo!' was heard in the June 2021 film *Mark, Mary & Some Other People*. The band acknowledged the track on Instagram in November and posted a YouTube video. The song is about partying through an apocalypse: similar to the first three songs on *¡Uno!*. The standalone singles show the band's improvement since their last album.

Live Albums

Live Tracks (1994)
This limited issue with just six tracks finds Green Day rocking out tracks from *Kerplunk* and *Dookie* Though 'One of My Lies' is a bit sloppy, there's an excellent performance of 'Chump'. It was included as a bonus disc of the tour edition of Dookie.

Bowling Bowling Bowling Parking Parking (1996)
This 7-song CD tracks their progress as a band live while on the tour promoting *Insomniac*. 'Brain Stew' is played faster, and 'Jaded' ridiculously fast. But Billie can't keep up singing, so they slow down a bit – people sing during the 'Knowledge' opening, still aware of the early track and 'Walking Contradiction' a bit faster.

Tune in, Tokyo (EP) (2001)
A seven song live EP issued in Japan originally and everywhere in 2014. It covers the tour promoting Warning. Armstrong is in a humorous mood, there's a fun reading of 'Minority' 'Waiting' is electric and Macy's Day Parade acoustic with electric accents, and a bigger beat.

Bullet In A Bible (2005)
By 2005, *American Idiot* had made major strides around the world. Green Day were renewed and reinvigorated with a new sound and a new look. They wore glitzy, fashionable outfits ditching the T-shirt and the tour was a significant boost to Green Day's standing in the music world. Green Day were total showmen and had been working together long enough to know how to get a crowd excited. To help, Green Day brought in their tour members Jason White on guitar and Jason Freese on numerous instruments, plus guests Ronnie Blake and Mike Pelino. *Bullet in a Bible* was issued on CD and DVD, but because Green Day had gradually extended the lengths of their shows over the years, the full shows were too long to be contained on a single CD. This is the only flaw of a tremendously enjoyable live album, although 'Jaded', 'Knowledge', 'Maria', 'We Are the Champions' and the magnum opus 'Homecoming' from the shows are missing. Much of *American Idiot* was played and many in the audience knew the songs well and even though they had a mountain of hit singles, they dropped a few of them in favor of their recent material. 'American Idiot' kicks off the concert in dazzling form, with its length extended for a brief crowd singalong. 'Jesus of Suburbia' is played masterfully for its nine-minute length. Billie Joe Armstrong introduced both Tré Coo after the first segment and Mike Dirnt after 'Dearly Beloved'. Both respond with nifty instrumentally charismatic moments.

'Are We the Waiting' and 'St. Jimmy' retain their album segue. 'Hitchin' a Ride' had Billie Joe working up the crowd as Mike plays the steady, bobbing bass line. Next up were some of Green Day's most popular 1990s classics played straight and great. The humorous 'King For a Day' is joined with 'Shout' though the crowd can't help being loud in the quiet section when Billie Joe asked them to shout a little less. The Isley Brothers classic is linked to Monty Python's 'Always Look on the Bright Side of Life'. The album ends much more quietly with 'Wake Me Up When September Ends', 'Boulevard of Broken Dreams' and an electrified version of 'Good Riddance'. 'Minority' adds life to this soft ending.

The album is loaded with stadium-shaking, monster performances that stop all over the fantastic, constantly singing fans. It was a major success hitting the top ten in several countries.

Last Night On Earth: Live in Tokyo' (EP) (2009)

A live EP release of tracks performed in Tokyo in 2009 in support of *21*st *Century Breakdown*, it matches up well with their later live CD, *Awesome As F**k*, which covers the same period. A few of the live tracks exclusive to this release can be combined with their 2011 live album to serve as an almost full Green Day concert circa 2009-2010. Mike Dirnt gets a long bass intro under Billie Joe Armstrong's vocals for 'Last of the American Girls', while '21 Guns' has a beautiful piano moment in the final verse by Jason Freese, 'American Eulogy' includes Dirnt's first sung lines on a live album and 'Geek Stink Breath' is a turbocharged version much faster than the original studio recording.

21 Guns Live (EP) (2009)

The '21 Guns' single was released in multiple versions, in multiple ways.

Awesome As F*ck (2011)

The CD has a mix of concert performances from various locations on their world tour supporting *21*st *Century Breakdown*. It's the only place to get the great song 'Cigarettes And Valentines,' since it's never been issued in strictly-audio form. Only 'Geek Stink Breath' from Saitama-Shi Japan is on the DVD version of this 2011 live CD.

Jason White, Jason Freese, and Jeff Matilka are on hand to help Green Day fill out their sound. The CD does a fine job of avoiding the live tracks from *Bullet in a Bible* with just three tracks duplicated. The CD's exclusive tracks missing from the DVD are: 'Going to Pasalacqua', 'J.A.R.', 'Who Wrote Holden Caufield?', 'American Idiot', and 'Wake Me Up When September Ends'.

'21 Century Breakdown' and 'Know Your Enemy' lead the charge. On the very first track, Billie Joe Armstrong directs the crowd, connecting well to the audience as usual, but it's not quite as effective without the visuals. 'Know Your Enemy' adds a chant and there's another great crowd moment on 'East Jesus Nowhere'. After a brief reminder of *American Idiot* with 'Holiday', 'Cigarettes and Valentines' is worked in and sits nicely next to some 1990s 'oldies' that storm in led by 'Burnout'. It wraps up softly with the ballads 'Wake Me Up When September Ends' and 'Good Riddance'. The live album reached #14 on the U.S. charts and hit #1 in the UK and a few other countries.

Live At Woodstock '94 (2019)

Green Day had hit the big time with this mud-slinging performance. They gained much initial fame from their 45-minute set as they poked fun at the mud-loving 1990s versions of hippies, and wound up with some of the most memorable moments of Woodstock '94.

Live At the Whisky (7" vinyl single) (2020)

The band posted two live playlists on their YouTube channel. *On The Radio* features some of their earliest live material, adding the unreleased song 'C Yo Yus.' Many of the tracks have never been issued in live form. The other live YouTube live playlist is *Scratch the Surface: Live 1994*, with 'Eye Of The Tiger/Paper Lanterns (Reprise)' being a previously unissued live track.

Compilations
1,039 Smoothed Out Slappy Hours (1991)
Compiles the *1000 Hours* EP, *39/Smooth* and the *Slappy* EP.

International Superhits! (2001)
A standard best-of collection with a second release of the 2000 B-side 'Maria,' and the exclusive 'Poprocks And Coke.'

Shenanigans (2002)
A standard B-sides collection with the new song 'Ha Ha You're Dead' closing the LP. It's Green Day's first album cover to feature their faces – but in graffiti form, spray-painted on a white wall.

Demolicious (2014)
A retry to get people more interested in the trilogy. There are 16 demos, the unreleased song 'State Of Shock' and an acoustic version of 'Stay The Night'.

'Greatest Hits: God's Favorite Band' (2017)
This second greatest hits album covers their entire career – meaning, it repeats songs featured on *International Superhits!* The exclusive tracks are a version of 'Ordinary World' with Miranda Lambert and the new track 'Back In the USA.' The album title stemmed from a joke by late-night talk show host Stephen Colbert.

Otis Big Guitar Mix (EP) (2020)
Another attempt by the band to give some attention to the trilogy. This features four of the songs in new mixes.

The band has released some reissue packages, like a collection of all their early albums, a singles collection, a box set that contains the 2012 trilogy, and the documentary *Cuatro!*

Nimrod 25 (2023)
This 5 CD/3 LP 25th anniversary Edition features a remaster of *Nimrod*, an album of contemporary demos and a 1997 concert from Philadelphia.

Videos

International Supervideos! (2001)
This DVD gathers all 15 Green Day music videos from 1994 to 2001.

Bullet in a Bible (2005)
This is an edited mix of two concerts performing to 130,000 people in total at Milton Keyes in Buckinghamshire, England. Only 14 of the 20 songs performed are present. Interview footage is interspersed throughout the live DVD version, but it would've been better to include the entire concert. The missing tracks are 'Jaded,' 'She,' 'Knowledge,' 'Maria,' 'Homecoming' and 'We Are The Champions.' Of these, 'Maria' and 'Homecoming' have never been issued in live versions. It matches the CD version, track for track.

'Awesome As Fuck' (2011)
This live DVD covering their 2009-2010 tour has a different track list than the CD version. The DVD was filmed in Saitama, Japan, but unfortunately – for a second time – the DVD was a truncated version of the performance. The DVD's tracks not found on CD are: 'Static Age', 'Boulevard of Broken Dreams', 'Welcome to Paradise', 'My Generation', 'American Eulogy', and 'Jesus of Suburbia'.

'Cigarettes And Valentines' (Live) (Lyrics: Armstrong; Music: Green Day)
This song is about Adrienne, and it's one of the songs that survived the mysterious disappearance of the studio tapes recorded after *Warning*. The song has a great melody, and energy that can be placed with their bombastic 2000s material or 1990s pop punk work. The vocal melody is the highlight, and Mike syncs with it for the chorus. Tré sticks to deeper toms here on the only released live Green Day song that was never issued in a studio version. It's some of both, and it rocks hard in its only released version. The lyric has Billie Joe inviting a woman on a date, to give her cigarettes and valentines.

Cuatro (2013)
The fourth instalment of the trilogy series features the band on the cover with new member Jason White. It's a documentary showing them creating *Uno!*, *Dos!* and *Tré!*.

Side Projects

Pinhead Gunpowder

Fanzine head and drummer Aaron Cometbus attempted to form a group called Pinhead Gunpowder in 1991. After a false start, he relocated and restarted the group, which included his friend Billie Joe Armstrong on lead vocals and guitar, Sara Kirsch on lead vocals and guitar, and Bill Schneider on bass and vocals. Future Green Day member Jason White replaced Kirsch on guitar and vocals in 1993. Between 1991 and 2009, they issued 8 punk EPs and an album.

The Network

Green Day never acknowledged that they were The Network in 2003 when they released the new wave *Money Money 2020*. In 2020, they issued *Money Money Part II: We Told Ya So* and the EP *Trans Am*. The musicians keep to their traditional instruments, but their names are changed. Armstrong is Fink, Dirnt is Van Gough, Tré Cool is The Snoo and Jason White is Balducci. Unknown player Captain Underpants plays keytar, and Z plays keyboards.

Foxboro Hot Tubs

Green Day formed this second side-project in 2007, to satisfy their garage-rock cravings. Armstrong is Reverend Strychnine Twitch, Dirnt is MIchaelangelo and Tré Cool is The Professor. They have help from Green Day touring member Jason Freese on keyboards, sax and flute, Frosco Lee on lead guitar, and Kevin Preston on rhythm guitar. They issued *Stop Drop and Roll!* in 2008. Without Green Day keeping it a secret, the album peaked at 21 in the US and 37 in the UK.

The Longshot

In 2018, Armstrong started another garage rock band for the album *Love Is For Losers* and four EPs. Kevin Preston from Foxboro Hot Tubs plays rhythm guitar, Jeff Matika plays bassist, and David S. Feld is the drummer.

The Coverups

In 2018, Armstrong Dirnt teamed up without Tré Cool for this cover band. They only play live and have released no music yet. The group is rounded out with ex-Green Day guitarist Jason White, bassist Bill Schneider from Pinhead Gunpowder, and drummer Chris Dugan.

Solo

Billie Joe Armstrong

After Armstrong's single 'Look Of Love' was issued in 1977, it was three decades before he issued an album under his own name. In 2013, he teamed up with pop singer Nora Jones for an Everly Brothers cover album named *Foreverly*. In 2020, he issued *No Fun Mondays* – a second covers album, but this time on his own. Amidst his side projects, he played bass for The Boo and The Shrives in the 2010s.

Mike Dirnt

Dirnt was involved in The Network and Foxboro Hot Tubs. He went off to other projects, like helping Screeching Weasel on bass and backing vocals in 1994, playing bass on one song for the band Squirtgun in 1995, and co-founded the new wave/punk band The Frustrators in 1999, playing bass and singing backing vocals. They released music through to 2011.

Tré Cool

Green Day noticed Tré when he played in The Lookouts. He also played the drums in Samiam in 1999. In 2018, he played with Dead Mermaids and Bubu And The Brood.

On Track series

Allman Brothers Band – Andrew Wild 978-1-78952-252-5
Tori Amos – Lisa Torem 978-1-78952-142-9
Asia – Peter Braidis 978-1-78952-099-6
Badfinger – Robert Day-Webb 978-1-878952-176-4
Barclay James Harvest – Keith and Monica Domone 978-1-78952-067-5
The Beatles – Andrew Wild 978-1-78952-009-5
The Beatles Solo 1969-1980 – Andrew Wild 978-1-78952-030-9
Blue Oyster Cult – Jacob Holm-Lupo 978-1-78952-007-1
Blur – Matt Bishop 978-178952-164-1
Marc Bolan and T.Rex – Peter Gallagher 978-1-78952-124-5
Kate Bush – Bill Thomas 978-1-78952-097-2
Camel – Hamish Kuzminski 978-1-78952-040-8
Captain Beefheart – Opher Goodwin 978-1-78952-235-8
Caravan – Andy Boot 978-1-78952-127-6
Cardiacs – Eric Benac 978-1-78952-131-3
Nick Cave and The Bad Seeds – Dominic Sanderson 978-1-78952-240-2
Eric Clapton Solo – Andrew Wild 978-1-78952-141-2
The Clash – Nick Assirati 978-1-78952-077-4
Crosby, Stills and Nash – Andrew Wild 978-1-78952-039-2
Creedence Clearwater Revival – Tony Thompson 978-178952-237-2
The Damned – Morgan Brown 978-1-78952-136-8
Deep Purple and Rainbow 1968-79 – Steve Pilkington 978-1-78952-002-6
Dire Straits – Andrew Wild 978-1-78952-044-6
The Doors – Tony Thompson 978-1-78952-137-5
Dream Theater – Jordan Blum 978-1-78952-050-7
Eagles – John Van der Kiste 978-1-78952-260-0
Electric Light Orchestra – Barry Delve 978-1-78952-152-8
Elvis Costello and The Attractions – Georg Purvis 978-1-78952-129-0
Emerson Lake and Palmer – Mike Goode 978-1-78952-000-2
Fairport Convention – Kevan Furbank 978-1-78952-051-4
Peter Gabriel – Graeme Scarfe 978-1-78952-138-2
Genesis – Stuart MacFarlane 978-1-78952-005-7
Gentle Giant – Gary Steel 978-1-78952-058-3
Gong – Kevan Furbank 978-1-78952-082-8
Hall and Oates – Ian Abrahams 978-1-78952-167-2
Hawkwind – Duncan Harris 978-1-78952-052-1
Peter Hammill – Richard Rees Jones 978-1-78952-163-4
Roy Harper – Opher Goodwin 978-1-78952-130-6
Jimi Hendrix – Emma Stott 978-1-78952-175-7
The Hollies – Andrew Darlington 978-1-78952-159-7
The Human League and The Sheffield Scene – Andrew Darlington 978-1-78952-186-3
Iron Maiden – Steve Pilkington 978-1-78952-061-3
Jefferson Airplane – Richard Butterworth 978-1-78952-143-6
Jethro Tull – Jordan Blum 978-1-78952-016-3
Elton John in the 1970s – Peter Kearns 978-1-78952-034-7
The Incredible String Band – Tim Moon 978-1-78952-107-8
Iron Maiden – Steve Pilkington 978-1-78952-061-3

Joe Jackson – Richard James 978-1-78952-189-4
Billy Joel – Lisa Torem 978-1-78952-183-2
Judas Priest – John Tucker 978-1-78952-018-7
Kansas – Kevin Cummings 978-1-78952-057-6
The Kinks – Martin Hutchinson 978-1-78952-172-6
Korn – Matt Karpe 978-1-78952-153-5
Led Zeppelin – Steve Pilkington 978-1-78952-151-1
Level 42 – Matt Philips 978-1-78952-102-3
Little Feat – Georg Purvis - 978-1-78952-168-9
Aimee Mann – Jez Rowden 978-1-78952-036-1
Joni Mitchell – Peter Kearns 978-1-78952-081-1
The Moody Blues – Geoffrey Feakes 978-1-78952-042-2
Motorhead – Duncan Harris 978-1-78952-173-3
Nektar – Scott Meze – 978-1-78952-257-0
New Order – Dennis Remmer – 979-1-78952-249-5
Laura Nyro – Philip Ward 978-1-78952-182-5
Mike Oldfield – Ryan Yard 978-1-78952-060-6
Opeth – Jordan Blum 978-1-78-952-166-5
Pearl Jam – Ben L. Connor 978-1-78952-188-7
Tom Petty – Richard James 978-1-78952-128-3
Pink Floyd – 978-1-78952-242-6 Richard Butterworth
Porcupine Tree – Nick Holmes 978-1-78952-144-3
Queen – Andrew Wild 978-1-78952-003-3
Radiohead – William Allen 978-1-78952-149-8
Rancid – Paul Matts 989-1-78952-187-0
Renaissance – David Detmer 978-1-78952-062-0
The Rolling Stones 1963-80 – Steve Pilkington 978-1-78952-017-0
The Smiths and Morrissey – Tommy Gunnarsson 978-1-78952-140-5
Spirit – Rev. Keith A. Gordon – 978-1-78952- 248-8
Stackridge – Alan Draper 978-1-78952-232-7
Status Quo the Frantic Four Years – Richard James 978-1-78952-160-3
Steely Dan – Jez Rowden 978-1-78952-043-9
Steve Hackett – Geoffrey Feakes 978-1-78952-098-9
Tears For Fears – Paul Clark - 978-178952-238-9
Thin Lizzy – Graeme Stroud 978-1-78952-064-4
Tool – Matt Karpe 978-1-78952-234-1
Toto – Jacob Holm-Lupo 978-1-78952-019-4
U2 – Eoghan Lyng 978-1-78952-078-1
UFO – Richard James 978-1-78952-073-6
Van Der Graaf Generator – Dan Coffey 978-1-78952-031-6
Van Halen – Morgan Brown – 9781-78952-256-3
The Who – Geoffrey Feakes 978-1-78952-076-7
Roy Wood and the Move – James R Turner 978-1-78952-008-8
Yes – Stephen Lambe 978-1-78952-001-9
Frank Zappa 1966 to 1979 – Eric Benac 978-1-78952-033-0
Warren Zevon – Peter Gallagher 978-1-78952-170-2
10CC – Peter Kearns 978-1-78952-054-5

Also available from Sonicbond

Decades Series
The Bee Gees in the 1960s – Andrew Môn Hughes et al 978-1-78952-148-1
The Bee Gees in the 1970s – Andrew Môn Hughes et al 978-1-78952-179-5
Black Sabbath in the 1970s – Chris Sutton 978-1-78952-171-9
Britpop – Peter Richard Adams and Matt Pooler 978-1-78952-169-6
Phil Collins in the 1980s – Andrew Wild 978-1-78952-185-6
Alice Cooper in the 1970s – Chris Sutton 978-1-78952-104-7
Curved Air in the 1970s – Laura Shenton 978-1-78952-069-9
Donovan in the 1960s – Jeff Fitzgerald 978-1-78952-233-4
Bob Dylan in the 1980s – Don Klees 978-1-78952-157-3
Brian Eno in the 1970s – Gary Parsons 978-1-78952-239-6
Faith No More in the 1990s – Matt Karpe 978-1-78952-250-1
Fleetwood Mac in the 1970s – Andrew Wild 978-1-78952-105-4
Fleetwood Mac in the 1980s – Don Klees 978-178952-254-9
Focus in the 1970s – Stephen Lambe 978-1-78952-079-8
Free and Bad Company in the 1970s – John Van der Kiste 978-1-78952-178-8
Genesis in the 1970s – Bill Thomas 978178952-146-7
George Harrison in the 1970s – Eoghan Lyng 978-1-78952-174-0
Kiss in the 1970s – Peter Gallagher 978-1-78952-246-4
Manfred Mann's Earth Band in the 1970s – John Van der Kiste 978178952-243-3
Marillion in the 1980s – Nathaniel Webb 978-1-78952-065-1
Van Morrison in the 1970s – Peter Childs - 978-1-78952-241-9
Mott the Hoople and Ian Hunter in the 1970s – John Van der Kiste 978-1-78-952-162-7
Pink Floyd In The 1970s – Georg Purvis 978-1-78952-072-9
Suzi Quatro in the 1970s – Darren Johnson 978-1-78952-236-5
Roxy Music in the 1970s – Dave Thompson 978-1-78952-180-1
Status Quo in the 1980s – Greg Harper 978-1-78952-244-0
Tangerine Dream in the 1970s – Stephen Palmer 978-1-78952-161-0
The Sweet in the 1970s – Darren Johnson 978-1-78952-139-9
Uriah Heep in the 1970s – Steve Pilkington 978-1-78952-103-0
Van der Graaf Generator in the 1970s – Steve Pilkington 978-1-78952-245-7
Yes in the 1980s – Stephen Lambe with David Watkinson 978-1-78952-125-2

On Screen series
Carry On… – Stephen Lambe 978-1-78952-004-0
David Cronenberg – Patrick Chapman 978-1-78952-071-2
Doctor Who: The David Tennant Years – Jamie Hailstone 978-1-78952-066-8
James Bond – Andrew Wild 978-1-78952-010-1
Monty Python – Steve Pilkington 978-1-78952-047-7
Seinfeld Seasons 1 to 5 – Stephen Lambe 978-1-78952-012-5

Other Books
1967: A Year In Psychedelic Rock 978-1-78952-155-9
1970: A Year In Rock – John Van der Kiste 978-1-78952-147-4
1973: The Golden Year of Progressive Rock 978-1-78952-165-8
Babysitting A Band On The Rocks – G.D. Praetorius 978-1-78952-106-1

Also available from Sonicbond

Eric Clapton Sessions – Andrew Wild 978-1-78952-177-1
Derek Taylor: For Your Radioactive Children – Andrew Darlington 978-1-78952-038-5
The Golden Road: The Recording History of The Grateful Dead – John Kilbride 978-1-78952-156-6
Iggy and The Stooges On Stage 1967-1974 – Per Nilsen 978-1-78952-101-6
Jon Anderson and the Warriors – the road to Yes – David Watkinson 978-1-78952-059-0
Misty: The Music of Johnny Mathis – Jakob Baekgaard 978-1-78952-247-1
Nu Metal: A Definitive Guide – Matt Karpe 978-1-78952-063-7
Tommy Bolin: In and Out of Deep Purple – Laura Shenton 978-1-78952-070-5
Maximum Darkness – Deke Leonard 978-1-78952-048-4
The Twang Dynasty – Deke Leonard 978-1-78952-049-1

and many more to come!

Would you like to write for Sonicbond Publishing?

At Sonicbond Publishing, we are always on the lookout for authors, particularly for our two main series. At the moment, we only accept books on music-related subjects.

On Track. Mixing fact with in-depth analysis, the On Track series examines the work of a particular musical artist or group. All genres are considered, from easy listening and jazz to 60s soul to 90s pop, via rock and metal.

Decades. An in-depth look at an important calendar decade in the career of a well-known artist or group.

While professional writing experience would, of course, be an advantage, the most important qualification is to have real enthusiasm and knowledge of your subject. First-time authors are welcomed, but the ability to write well in English is essential.

Sonicbond Publishing has distribution throughout Europe, North America and Australia and all books will also published in E-book form. Authors will be paid a royalty based on sales.

Further details are available from www.sonicbondpublishing.co.uk.

To get in touch, complete the contact form there or email info@sonicbondpublishing.co.uk

Follow us on social media:
Twitter: https://twitter.com/SonicbondP
Instagram: https://www.instagram.com/sonicbondpublishing_/
Facebook: https://www.facebook.com/SonicbondPublishing/

Linktree QR code: